The EXPERT VEGETABLE NOTEBOOK

Dr. D.G. Hessayon

Year:	Location:

First Edition: 60,000 copies

Published by Expert Books
a division of Transworld Publishers

Copyright © Dr. D. G. Hessayon 2009

The right of Dr. D. G. Hessayon to be identified
as author of this work has been asserted in accordance with sections
77 and 78 of the Copyright Designs and Patents Act 1988.

A catalogue record for this book is available from the British Library

TRANSWORLD PUBLISHERS
61-63 Uxbridge Road, London W5 5SA
a division of the Random House Group Ltd

EXPERT BOOKS

Reproduction by Spot On Digital Imaging Ltd, Gomm Road, High Wycombe, Bucks HP13 7DJ
Printed and bound by Mohn Media Mohndruck GmbH

ISBN 978 0 903505 76 5

© D.G.HESSAYON 2009

CHAPTER 1

INTRODUCTION

How to use this book

On each page you will find scores of facts to help you with your plants. Check up each time you decide to buy or have a new job to do. On many of the pages there are sections which are printed in blue — these are for you to fill in with your own information. In this way you can build up a permanent record and a useful reminder for next year.

Raising your own vegetables has a fascination for millions of men and women throughout the country. You can save money by growing vegetables — it has been estimated that an expenditure of £1 yields crops worth £12 or more at shop prices. But saving money is not the main motive for most people — there are more important reasons for growing food in the garden.

First of all there is the enjoyment of an active and healthy hobby — plus the satisfaction of eating the product of your own labour. In addition there are more practical benefits. The crop can be harvested at the peak of tenderness and flavour instead of having to wait for maximum yields like the professional grower. You can grow vegetables which never appear in the shops and you can grow top-flavour varieties of ordinary vegetables which farmers never grow. You can also serve vegetables within an hour or two of picking and with sweet corn, asparagus, chicory, beans etc that means a new flavour experience.

It takes a well-run plot of about 1,000 sq.ft to keep one person supplied with all his or her vegetable requirements (except potatoes) for a whole year. At the end of the scale a few tubs or growing bags on a patio can provide fresh tomatoes, french beans, courgettes and new potatoes. Either way, there is the thrill of growing your own.

CROP ROTATION

You should not grow a vegetable in the same spot year after year. If you do then soil troubles are likely to build up, and the level of nutrients will become unbalanced. Crop rotation is the answer, and the standard 3 year plan is shown here. A strip of land at one end of the plot is sometimes used for permanent crops (rhubarb, asparagus etc) and is left out of the plan. Not everyone is willing to follow this rotation plan, and regrettably all idea of a rotation is abandoned. It would be much better to follow a very simple rotation — roots this year, above-ground crops next year and then back to root crops.

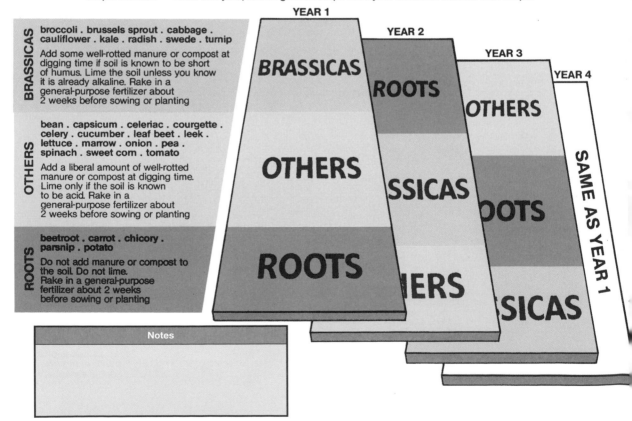

BRASSICAS

broccoli . brussels sprout . cabbage . cauliflower . kale . radish . swede . turnip

Add some well-rotted manure or compost at digging time if soil is known to be short of humus. Lime the soil unless you know it is already alkaline. Rake in a general-purpose fertilizer about 2 weeks before sowing or planting

OTHERS

bean . capsicum . celeriac . courgette . celery . cucumber . leaf beet . leek . lettuce . marrow . onion . pea . spinach . sweet corn . tomato

Add a liberal amount of well-rotted manure or compost at digging time. Lime only if the soil is known to be acid. Rake in a general-purpose fertilizer about 2 weeks before sowing or planting

ROOTS

beetroot . carrot . chicory . parsnip . potato

Do not add manure or compost to the soil. Do not lime. Rake in a general-purpose fertilizer about 2 weeks before sowing or planting

Notes

1 in. = 2.5 cm, 1 ft = 30 cm, 1 oz = 28 gm, 1 lb = 450 gm

BASIC RULES

 DIG EARLY

Don't try to dig and make a seed bed in one operation. The time for digging is during a dry spell in late autumn or early winter if you intend to sow or plant in the spring. Choose a spade which is suited to your height and strength — keep the blade clean. Begin slowly — about 30 minutes is quite enough for the first day. Insert the blade vertically, not at an angle. Leave the soil in lumps — frost will break down the clods during winter.

Digging Notes

 PREPARE A PROPER SEED BED

In early spring the soil will become workable — moist but not sticky. Now is the time to make a seed bed. The first job is to break down the clods — use a hand cultivator or a garden fork, working on a push-pull principle across the surface. Now rake in a dressing of fertilizer and then walk over the surface with a rake, using the implement and not your feet to fill in the hollows and break down the mounds. Pick up debris and small stones. The final step is to use the rake in a push-pull fashion to produce a smooth and level seed bed with a crumbly surface.

 BUY GOOD QUALITY SEEDS & PLANTS

Always obtain good quality seed, and don't leave ordering to the last minute. Store the packets inside a tin with a tight lid in a cool place. Sometimes you will need to buy seedlings instead of seeds for transplanting into the plot. Choose carefully — the plants should be sturdy, green and with a good root system. Here you *should* leave it to the last minute, because there must be a minimum delay between purchase and planting.

Buying Notes

 SOW NON-STORABLE CROPS LITTLE & OFTEN

Several vegetables such as lettuce, radish and cabbage cannot be stored for later use. To avoid gluts and famines it is wise to sow a short row every few weeks. A boon for the busy (or lazy) gardener are the 'mixed seed' packets of lettuce, radish etc offered by many seed suppliers. The mixture of early- and late-maturing varieties gives a protracted harvesting period from a single sowing.

 SOW & PLANT AT THE PROPER TIME

Proper timing is extremely important. The calendars in this book will give you the approximate times for sowing and planting — soil and weather conditions determine the exact time. The soil must be moist but it must not be wet and waterlogged. Remember the basic seed sowing rule — not too early, not too deeply, not too thickly. The traditional method is to sow the seed in drills, marking the ends with sticks. In recent years the bed system has become increasingly popular — the seeds are sown in a block rather than in drills so that all plants are the same distance from each other. Spacings are quite close so that the leaves of mature plants touch each other.

 THIN PROMPTLY & ENSURE RAPID GROWTH

Remove weeds and thin the seedlings as soon after germination as practical. Overcrowding at this early stage can be crippling. Firm the plants after thinning and gently water to settle the disturbed roots. The growing plants must be watered and fed if necessary to ensure rapid growth. Water shortage and starvation are common causes of leathery leaves, premature running to seed, woody roots and lack of flavour.

 TACKLE PROBLEMS PROMPTLY

Inspect the plants regularly and at the first sign of trouble look up the cause on page 58. For a more detailed description of vegetable troubles consult The Vegetable Expert. Once you have put a name to the problem, act quickly. Many pests and diseases can be checked quite easily if treated promptly, but may be difficult or impossible to control if left to get out of hand. It is a good idea to keep a small selection of pesticides in the garden shed for emergency use. Keep them away from children and read the instructions before spraying.

 PICK MOST CROPS EARLY & OFTEN

You may be surprised at some of the harvesting times recommended in this book — turnips the size of a golf ball and carrots no longer than a finger. But the young stage is often the peak time for tenderness and flavour. With some crops such as marrows, cucumber, peas and beans it is essential to pick regularly as just a few mature fruits or pods left on the plant can bring cropping to an end.

BASIC RULES

Vegetable	Easy or difficult	Number of seeds per ounce	Expected germination time	Life expectancy of seed	Time from sowing to harvest	Time from planting to harvest	Page number
ARTICHOKE, GLOBE	Not easy — needs space & attention	—	—	—	—	1½ years	8
ASPARAGUS	Not easy — needs space & attention	—	—	—	—	2 years	9
BEAN, BROAD	Easy	15	7–14 days	2 years	Spring sowing: 14 weeks Autumn sowing: 26 weeks	—	10–11
BEAN, FRENCH	Easy	60	7–14 days	2 years	8–12 weeks	—	12–13
BEAN, RUNNER	Easy, but support & constant picking necessary	30	7–14 days	2 years	12–14 weeks	8–10 weeks	14–15
BEET, LEAF	Easy	2000	10–14 days	3 years	12 weeks	—	16
BEETROOT	Easy	2000	10–14 days	3 years	Globe vars: 11 weeks Long vars: 16 weeks	—	17
BROCCOLI	Moderately easy	8000	7–12 days	4 years	Green vars: 16 weeks Other vars: 44 weeks	Green vars: 10 weeks Other vars: 38 weeks	18
BRUSSELS SPROUT	Moderately easy if soil is suitable	8000	7–12 days	4 years	Early vars: 28 weeks Late vars: 36 weeks	Early vars: 22 weeks Late vars: 30 weeks	19
CABBAGE	Moderately easy	8000	7–12 days	4 years	Spring vars: 35 weeks Summer vars: 20 weeks	Spring vars: 29 weeks Summer vars: 14 weeks	20–21
CAPSICUM	Difficult	4000	14–21 days	5 years	18 weeks	10 weeks	22
CARROT	Moderately difficult	20,000	17 days	4 years	Early vars: 12 weeks Maincrop vars: 16 weeks	—	23
CAULIFLOWER	Difficult	8000	7–12 days	4 years	Summer vars: 18 weeks Winter vars: 46 weeks	Summer vars: 12 weeks Winter vars: 40 weeks	24–25
CELERIAC	Moderately difficult	70,000	12–18 days	5 years	35 weeks	28 weeks	26
CELERY	Difficult	70,000	12–18 days	5 years	Trench vars: 40 weeks Self-blanching vars: 25 weeks	Trench vars: 32 weeks Self-blanching vars: 17 weeks	27
CHICORY	Moderately easy	20,000	7–14 days	5 years	18–30 weeks	—	28
COURGETTE	Moderately easy	150	5–8 days	6 years	10 weeks	8 weeks	29

Vegetable	Easy or difficult	Number of seeds per ounce	Expected germination time	Life expectancy of seed	Time from sowing to harvest	Time from planting to harvest	Page number
CUCUMBER, GREENHOUSE	Difficult	75	3–5 days	6 years	14 weeks	10 weeks	30
CUCUMBER, OUTDOOR	Difficult	75	6–9 days	6 years	14 weeks	12 weeks	31
KALE	Easy	8000	7–12 days	4 years	35 weeks	29 weeks	32
LEEK	Easy, but occupies land for a long time	10,000	14–18 days	3 years	Early vars: 30 weeks Late vars: 45 weeks	Early vars: 22 weeks Late vars: 37 weeks	33
LETTUCE	Moderately easy if rules are followed	20,000	6–12 days	3 years	8–14 weeks	—	34–35
MARROW, SQUASH & PUMPKIN	Moderately easy	150	5–8 days	6 years	14 weeks	12 weeks	36
ONION & SHALLOT from sets	Easy	Onion: 5 Shallot: 2	Sprout in 11–14 days	—	—	18–20 weeks	37
ONION from seed	Moderately easy if proper seed bed is prepared	8000	21 days	1–2 years	Spring-sown vars: 22 weeks Summer-sown vars: 46 weeks	—	38–39
PARSNIP	Easy	8000	10–28 days	1 year	34 weeks	—	40
PEA	Difficult	75	7–10 days	2 years	12–16 weeks	—	41–43
POTATO	Moderately easy	½–1 seed potato	Sprout in 6 weeks	—	—	Early vars: 13 weeks Maincrop vars: 22 weeks	44–45
RADISH	Easy	3000	4–7 days	6 years	Summer vars: 3–6 weeks Winter vars: 10–12 weeks	—	46
SPINACH	Moderately easy if rules are followed	1500	12–20 days	4 years	8–14 weeks	—	47
SWEDE	Easy	8000	6–10 days	3 years	20–24 weeks	—	48
SWEET CORN	Moderately easy in right location	100	10–12 days	2 years	14 weeks	—	49
TOMATO, GREENHOUSE	Moderately difficult	7000	8–11 days	3 years	20 weeks	12 weeks	50–51
TOMATO, OUTDOOR	Difficult	7000	8–11 days	3 years	20 weeks	12 weeks	52–53
TURNIP	Easy	8000	6–10 days	3 years	6–12 weeks	—	54

VEGETABLE PLOT PLAN

Draw the outline of your plot and mark the position of the rows on the plan. Write in the names of the vegetables along the lines. Alternatively you can note each reference (e.g D-6 to N-6) on the appropriate page of the A–Z guide.

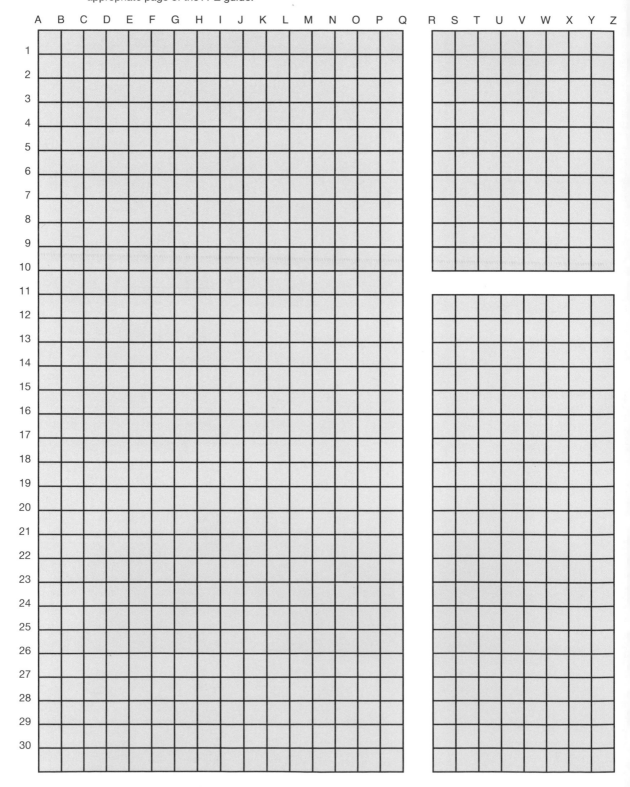

CHAPTER 2
VEGETABLES A–Z

VARIETIES These are not necessarily the "best" varieties — they have been chosen on the basis of their popularity in catalogues, shops and stores

YIELD The yield which can be expected under average growing conditions

TYPES Basic groups into which the varieties are divided

VEGETABLES A–Z

BEETROOT

page 7

An easy vegetable which will grow in any reasonable soil. Rather slow to start, but growth is rapid once the seedlings are through. The secret is to avoid any check to growth and to pull the roots before they are large. There are 3 types — the popular globe, the less common cylindrical and the exhibitor-only long. 'Seeds' of standard varieties are corky fruits containing several true seeds. Monogerm varieties produce one seedling per seed.

Harvesting

Pull out roots of globe varieties as required. Twist off (do not cut) leaves. Roots grown for storage should be lifted in October. Shake off soil and discard damaged roots. Place the roots between layers of dry peat in a box and store in a shed. The crop will keep until March.

When the seedlings are about 1 in. high, thin out to leave a single plant at each station. Protection against birds may be necessary. The ground must be kept weed-free. Dryness leads to woodiness — a sudden return to wet conditions leads to splitting, so avoid problems water moderately every fortnight during dry spells.

Pull up alternate plants when roots reach golf-ball size — use for cooking. Leave the remainder to reach maturity.

Varieties

BOLTARDY: Widely available — the usual choice for early sowing. Deep red flesh

MONODET: A monogerm variety — crimson-fleshed and free from rings

MONOPOLY: A monogerm variety — noted for its flavour and resistance to woodiness

DETROIT-LITTLE BALL: A favourite choice for late sowing. Produces 'baby' beets for pickling

DETROIT-CRIMSON GLOBE: The standard choice for later planting — an old favourite

DETROIT-NEW GLOBE: A good choice for exhibiting. Uniform shape, ring-free flesh

BURPEE'S GOLDEN: The skin is orange, and the yellow flesh does not bleed when cut

ALBINA VEREDUNA: The most popular white variety. Leaves can be cooked as greens

CYLINDRA: An oval beet with excellent keeping qualities. Deep red flesh

RONO: Full-grown roots are an ideal size — long and 2 in. across

CHELTENHAM GREEN TOP: The most popular highly recommended Long variety

CHELTENHAM MONO: A monogerm variety — recommended for showing and winter storage

SPRINTER

	Shape & colour	Bolt★ resistant	Variety grown	Yield, flavour & notes for next year	Expected yield
		YES			
		YES			
		YES			
		NO			
		NO	✓		
		NO			
		NO			
		NO			
		NO			
		NO			
		YES			

Globe varieties: 18 lb from a 10 ft row
Long varieties: 18 lb from a 10 ft row

Same trouble as last year — the plants ran to seed. The roots were rather woody — will try Sprinter next year!

★ Variety which will not readily run to seed in poor growing conditions

Calendar

An early crop which will be ready in late May or June, sow a bolt-resistant variety under glass in a frame in early March.

The main sowing period begins outdoors in mid March. Sowing of globe varieties in mid May gives a regular supply. Sow Long varieties in mid May for winter storage — tender roots.

For roots from earliest sowings may be too sowing time in October sowings may be too late. For autumn crop sow Detroit-Little Ball in July.

	JAN	FEB	MAR	APR	MAY	JUN	JUL	AUG	SEP	OCT	NOV	DEC
Recommended Sowing Time												
Actual Sowing Dates												
Expected Lifting Time												
Actual Lifting Dates				4								
								21	10			

For key to symbols — see page 7

CALENDAR

	Most popular time for sowing or planting outdoors
	Less usual time for sowing or planting outdoors. The earlier panel generally refers to S. England
	Recommended time for sowing outdoors under cloches or in a cold frame
	Recommended time for sowing indoors under glass
	Recommended time for transplanting seedlings raised under glass
	Recommended time for transplanting seedlings raised under glass. Cover with cloches
	Recommended time for transplanting seedlings raised under glass into pots/bags in the greenhouse
	Most popular time for harvesting
	Less usual time for harvesting

Write in the name of an unlisted variety which you are growing or propose to grow in the garden. The fact that a variety is not listed means that it is not offered by many suppliers – it does not necessarily mean that it is a poor choice

Mark the variety you are growing with a red tick. Use a pencil to tick a variety which you propose to try in the future

Note down your views on performance. In case of a poor showing check in The Vegetable Expert to see if you are doing something wrong. It may be time to try a new variety

4 June — the date seed was sown this year

21 September — the date the first roots were lifted for kitchen use

10 October — the date the roots were lifted for storage

ARTICHOKE, GLOBE

Seed Sowing

Raising plants from seed is possible but not advisable. Sow thinly in drills which are 1 in. deep and 1 ft apart. Thin the seedlings — they should be about 9 in. apart in the rows. Plant out in the following spring.

Planting

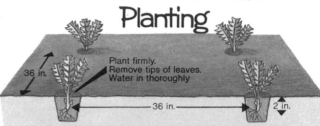

Plant firmly.
Remove tips of leaves.
Water in thoroughly

36 in.

36 in.

2 in.

This vegetable requires a permanent plot — it is more at home in the herbaceous border than in the vegetable plot. It is tall (3–4 ft high) and thistle-like — the arching silvery leaves provide an attractive foil for the bright floral display. It is a fussy plant in many ways, requiring good soil, regular watering, liberal manuring and frost protection in winter. Globe artichokes are usually grown from offsets (rooted suckers) rather than seed. These offsets are taken from either high-yielding plants in the garden or are bought from a garden centre. Roots must be attached and the ideal height is 9 in.

Good drainage is essential — it is a waste of time to grow this crop in heavy clay. Dig the soil in autumn and incorporate compost or well-rotted manure.

Plant as shown above — keep the plants well watered until established. Apply a mulch in May.

During the summer months hoe regularly and apply a liquid fertilizer at fortnightly intervals. Water thoroughly when the weather is dry. Keep watch for aphids and slugs — treat at the first signs of attack.

In late autumn cut down the stems and cover the crowns with bracken, leaves, straw or bark chips. Remove this protective covering in April.

Harvesting

A few small heads will begin to form in the first year — cut off immediately and discard. Cropping begins in the season after planting — the ball-like heads are removed for boiling just before the fleshy scales open. Remove the terminal bud ('kinghead') first, leaving 2–3 in. of stem attached. Feed the plants after this initial cropping — later in the season remove and cook the smaller secondary heads.

Varieties

	Variety grown	Yield, flavour & notes for next year	Expected yield
GREEN GLOBE: The only variety you are likely to find in the seed catalogues. Thick, fleshy scales — can be bought as offsets for planting			
PURPLE GLOBE ROMANESCO: The most popular of the purple varieties. The heads are smaller than Green Globe, but the flavour is better			
VERT DE LAON: This one is bought as offsets for planting rather than grown from seed. Compact plants — excellent flavour			10–12 heads per mature plant
CAMUS DE BRETAGNE: The heads are large and the flavour is good, but it is a rarity. Not suitable for northern counties			
VIOLETTA DI CHIOGGIA: A purple-headed variety to raise from seed for the herbaceous border. Rogue out green-headed plants			

Calendar

Do not plant too many — just 2 or 3 plants will generally provide enough heads for your family.

April is the best month for sowing seeds and for planting offsets.

The plants will not last forever — plant rooted offsets each spring so that mature specimens can be disposed of after a few years.

	JAN	FEB	MAR	APR	MAY	JUN	JUL	AUG	SEP	OCT	NOV	DEC
Recommended Sowing Time												
Actual Sowing Dates												
Recommended Planting Time												
Actual Planting Dates												
Expected Cutting Time												
Actual Cutting Dates												

1 in. = 2.5 cm, 1 ft = 30 cm, 1 oz = 28 gm, 1 lb = 450 gm

For key to symbols — see page 7

ASPARAGUS

Seed Sowing

Raising plants from seed is possible, but buying crowns from a garden centre or mail order company is much more popular. Sow seed thinly in drills which are 1 in. deep and 1 ft apart. Thin the seedlings when they are 3 in. tall — they should be about 6 in. apart in the rows. Plant out in the following spring.

There are two things you will need to grow asparagus successfully — patience and free-draining soil. Patience because you will have to wait until the second year after planting before cutting your first spears — free-draining soil because the fleshy roots soon rot when waterlogged. There are lots of old wives' tales concerning this crop, but in fact you don't need wide spacing, heavy annual dressings of manure nor a regular sprinkling of salt. Thorough soil preparation and careful planting are essential and your reward is a bed of a luxury vegetable which should stay productive for 10–20 years. Asparagus is nearly always raised from rooted plants ('crowns') rather than from seed.

Planting

Keep roots covered under sacking until planting time — never let them dry out

Cover crowns with 2 in. of sifted soil immediately after spreading out roots. Fill in trench gradually as plants grow — bed should be level by autumn

8 in.
3 in.
12 in.

Pick a sunny spot sheltered from strong winds. Dig the soil in autumn and incorporate a liberal amount of compost or well-rotted manure. Remove the roots of all perennial weeds during soil preparation.

Plant as shown above — these days you can buy asparagus plants in peat blocks and these are simply planted with a trowel and covered with about 2 in. of soil. Keep the beds weed-free and well watered during dry weather. In summer remove berries before they fall to the ground and in autumn cut down the ferny stems once they have turned yellow. The stumps should be 1–2 in. above the surface.

In subsequent years make a ridge of soil with a draw hoe over each row before the spears appear in spring.

Harvesting

Do not cut any spears in the year of planting nor in the following year. Cutting can begin in the second year after planting. As soon as the spears reach a height of 4–5 in. they should be severed about 3 in. below the soil surface. Use a long serrated kitchen knife. Cut every day if necessary. In early or mid June you must stop cutting so that the spears can develop into the ferny stems which build up the food reserves for next year's crop.

Varieties

	Sex of plants	Variety grown	Yield, flavour & notes for next year	Expected yield
CONNOVERS COLOSSAL: Still the most popular variety, available as seed or crowns. Thick-stalked, crops early and is excellent for freezing	M & F			
MARTHA WASHINGTON: A long-established U.S. variety which produces long spears in early June. Rust-resistant and reliable	M & F			
STEWART'S PURPLE: A variety which is unusually low in stringy fibre and has a purple colour which does not fade when cooked	M & F			
GIJNLIM: A modern star which has outperformed many other types in trials and is noted for its earliness	M			
JERSEY KNIGHT: Good quality spears — up to 1 in. thick with good disease resistance. No seed-producing female plants	M			20–25 spears per mature plant

M & F *Plants may be male or female*
M *All-male — male plants are stronger than female ones*

Calendar

Use 1-year-old crowns. You can buy 2- or 3-year-old crowns but they can be temperamental.

Plant crowns´ in early April if the soil is in good condition — delay for a couple of weeks if the weather is cold and wet. Trenches should be dug about 3 ft apart.

Harvesting of the mature crop takes place over a 6–8 week period. To ensure the maximum harvest period, plant a mixed bed containing an early variety such as Connovers Colossal with a later variety such as Martha Washington.

	JAN	FEB	MAR	APR	MAY	JUN	JUL	AUG	SEP	OCT	NOV	DEC
Recommended Sowing Time												
Actual Sowing Dates												
Recommended Planting Time												
Actual Planting Dates												
Expected Cutting Time												
Actual Cutting Dates												

1 in. = 2.5 cm, 1 ft = 30 cm, 1 oz = 28 gm, 1 lb = 450 gm

For key to symbols — see page 7

BEAN, BROAD

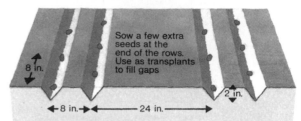

Sow a few extra seeds at the end of the rows. Use as transplants to fill gaps

8 in.

8 in. — 24 in. — 2 in.

Nearly any soil can produce an adequate crop, although the ideal soil is rich and free-draining. Few vegetables are easier to grow, and these are the first garden beans to grace your table. Picking can begin as early as the end of May if you have pampered the crop, but even the maincrop sown in the ordinary way in early April will be ready for harvest in July.

Hoe regularly to keep down weeds when the plants are small. Watering will not be needed at this stage, but you will have to water copiously in dry weather when the pods are swelling.

Support is necessary for tall-growing varieties. Place a stout cane at each corner of the double row and then stretch twine between these canes.

Pinch off the top 3 in. of stem as soon as the first pods start to form. This will ensure an earlier crop and also provide some degree of blackfly control. This serious pest must be kept down, so spray with an insecticide if attacks persist.

Harvesting

Do not leave the pods to reach their maximum size — the beans inside will be tough. Begin picking when the first pods are 2–3 in. long — cook them whole.

The time to pick for shelling is when the beans have begun to show through the pod but before the scar on each shelled bean has become discoloured. Remove the pod with a sharp downward twist.

Types

LONGPOD varieties (L)

The long, narrow pods hang downwards, reaching 15 in. or more in length. There are 8–10 kidney-shaped beans within each pod — both green and white varieties are available. This is the best group for hardiness, early cropping, exhibiting and top yields.

WINDSOR varieties (W)

The pods are shorter and broader than those of the main group — the Longpods. There are 4–7 round beans within each pod — both green and white varieties are available. This is the best group for flavour. They are not suitable for autumn sowing and they take longer to mature than Longpods.

DWARF varieties (D)

The dwarf, freely-branching bushes grow about 12–18 in. high, making them the ideal choice where tall growth is not required or the site is exposed. These are the broad beans to choose for growing under cloches.

Calendar

There are several ways of growing a crop which will be ready for picking in June. November sowing (Aquadulce or The Sutton) will provide beans in early June, but there can be serious losses in a severe winter. Only attempt autumn sowing if your plot is sheltered, free-draining and located in a mild area. It is a better plan to sow under cloches in February.

Maincrop sowings begin in March and then at monthly intervals until the end of May to provide beans throughout the summer.

	JAN	FEB	MAR	APR	MAY	JUN	JUL	AUG	SEP	OCT	NOV	DEC
Recommended Sowing Time												
Actual Sowing Dates												
Expected Picking Time												
Actual Picking Dates												

1 in. = 2.5 cm, 1 ft = 30 cm, 1 oz = 28 gm, 1 lb = 450 gm

For key to symbols — see page 7

Varieties

	Type	Bean colour	Variety grown	Yield, flavour & notes for next year	Expected yield
AQUADULCE CLAUDIA: This is the standard variety for autumn sowing. Tall, prolific and very hardy. A good choice for freezing	L				
IMPERIAL GREEN LONGPOD: A tall high-yielding variety with extra-long pods. Good disease resistance — suitable for exhibition	L				
RELON: Vigorous and reliable. Pods over 20 in. with 10–11 beans have been claimed. Good for freezing and showing	L				
IMPERIAL WHITE LONGPOD: An old favourite with a good reputation for high yields and medals at shows. Hard to find	L				
HYLON: One of the white-bean varieties which produces longer pods than its rivals. Highly recommended for exhibition and freezing	L				
BUNYARD'S EXHIBITION: Still in some catalogues although it's not the biggest nor longest nor tastiest. Just thoroughly reliable	L				
MASTERPIECE LONGPOD: A widely available variety with fine-flavoured green beans. Sow in February or March — crops early	L				
EXPRESS: Well named — it is one of the fastest maturing of all broad beans. Sow in early spring for a midsummer crop	L				
RED EPICURE: Not easy to find, but quite different from any other. Beans turn yellow when cooked — flavour quite distinctive	L				
DREADNOUGHT: A Longpod which is recommended for exhibiting as the pods are well-shaped and extraordinarily long. Hard to find	L				
MEDES: Medium-sized pods are borne on 3ft-high plants. This broad bean is recommended for spring planting. Good freezing variety	L				
WITKIEM MANITA: It is claimed that this broad bean can crop as early as the autumn-sown varieties and give higher yields	L				
COLOSSAL: A good culinary variety — the beans are plump and fine-flavoured. Pods are long and well-shaped — hard to find	L				
GREEN WINDSOR: Heavy-cropping and perhaps the best-tasting broad bean — but it is now hard to find. It is the parent of many other varieties	W				
JUBILEE HYSOR: An early-cropping Windsor type with an excellent flavour. The young pods can be cooked whole	W				
THE SUTTON: The most popular of the Dwarf varieties — much praise has been heaped on it. Can be sown in March-June or November	D				
BONNY LAD: Introduced as a rival to The Sutton but no longer popular. Grows taller (18 in. compared to 12 in.) Pods 5 in. long	D				
OPTICA: This compact variety is taller than The Sutton but is still a good choice for the little garden. The pods are small	D				
					20 lb from a 10 ft double row

L Longpod variety
W Windsor variety
D Dwarf variety

1 in. = 2.5 cm, 1 ft = 30 cm, 1 oz = 28 gm, 1 lb = 450 gm

VEGETABLES A-Z

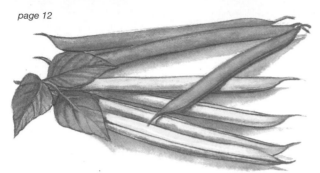

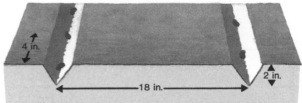

BEAN, FRENCH

The french bean is a half hardy annual which cannot stand frost. Do not plant before the recommended time — seed will rot in cold and wet soil. If space is short grow them in the flower garden — the bushy plants bear white, pink or red flowers and varieties are available with brightly-coloured pods. An easy crop, provided the site is not heavy clay and is reasonably sunny.

Harvesting

A pod is ready for picking if it snaps easily when bent but before the tell-tale bulges of maturity are present. Pick several times a week if necessary — you can expect to continue cropping for 5–7 weeks.

Take care not to loosen the plant when harvesting — hold the stems when tugging away the pods, or use a pair of scissors.

Hoe regularly to keep down weeds when the plants are small. Support the plants with short twigs or pea sticks. Use poles, netting or twiggy branches for climbing varieties.

Spraying the flowers is not necessary to ensure that they will set properly. Moisture at the roots, however, is essential to ensure maximum pod development and a long cropping period. Water copiously and regularly if the weather turns dry during or after the flowering period.

Slugs can be a problem, especially with seedlings, and aphids often attack the plants in summer. Treat at the first signs of trouble. Halo blight can be a problem in a wet season — brown leaf spots with a yellow halo. Unfortunately there is no cure.

Types

Most french beans are **Bush** varieties, growing as compact branching plants 12–18 in. high. There are a few **Climbing** varieties which will clamber up a support to a height of 5 ft or more. The usual pod colour is green, but you can also buy yellow and purple varieties — there is even a striped one for the novelty seeker. The coloured pod has a practical advantage — the pods can be easily seen at picking time.

FLAT-POD varieties (F)

Before the War these varieties dominated the catalogues. They are the 'English' varieties — flat, rather wide and often with a tendency to become stringy as they mature. You will find the old favourites here, but there are some new stringless varieties such as Limelight.

PENCIL-POD varieties (P)

The catalogues are now dominated by these 'Continental' varieties — round and generally stringless. Small pods are usually cooked whole.

French beans are nearly always eaten in the fresh green pod state — the 'haricot vert' of the French. With some varieties (Chevrier Vert is the notable example) the fresh bean ('flageolet') can be removed from the pods and cooked, or dried ('haricot') for cooking later.

Calendar

	JAN	FEB	MAR	APR	MAY	JUN	JUL	AUG	SEP	OCT	NOV	DEC
Recommended Sowing Time				▨	▨	▨						
Actual Sowing Dates												
Expected Picking Time							▨	▨	▨	▨		
Actual Picking Dates												

For an early crop sow a quick-maturing variety in early May. If you want to pick beans before the end of June then you will have to grow the plants under cloches. Put the cloches in position in early March and sow the seeds in the soil beneath them in early or mid April. Remove the cloches in late May.

The maincrop is sown during May. Successional sowings up to the end of June will provide pods until early October.

For a late autumn crop sow in July and cover the plants with cloches in mid September.

1 in. = 2.5 cm, 1 ft = 30 cm, 1 oz = 28 gm, 1 lb = 450 gm

For key to symbols — see page 7

Varieties

Varieties	Type	Pod colour	Variety grown	Yield, flavour & notes for next year	Expected yield
THE PRINCE: A popular variety — you will find it in many catalogues. Dwarf-growing — pick pods when young. Good for exhibiting	F/B				
MASTERPIECE: A long-established variety — suitable for early sowing and growing under cloches. Pods are long and straight	F/B				
CANADIAN WONDER: Once a favourite Flat-pod but it is no longer in the popular catalogues. A heavy cropper, but it fell out of favour	F/B				
LIMELIGHT: The thick pods are broad and stringless. It is claimed to be one of the earliest french beans, and the flavour is sweet. Hard to find	F/B				
BORLOTTO: A real novelty. Both the young pods and the beans are pale green with bright red stripes and blotches	F/B				
HUNTER: Noted for its large pods and heavy crops — a popular Continental variety. Suitable for growing outdoors or under glass. Stringless	F/C				
TENDERGREEN: Once the most popular Pencil-pod variety. It has many good points — stringless, early, prolific and recommended for freezing	P/B				
COBRA: A modern replacement for Blue Lake. An attractive variety — mauve flowers and long, straight pods. Black-seeded	P/B				
CROPPER TEEPEE: A white-seeded variety with just one outstanding advantage — the pods are borne well above the leaves for easy picking	P/B				
RADAR: Another very slender bean — pick pods at 4 in. stage and cook whole. It is a heavy-cropping variety with a good flavour. Hard to find	P/B				
SAFARI: Low-growing but vigorous — the slender straight pods are stringless. A reliable plant with good disease resistance. Pods held above foliage	P/B				
OPERA: A heavy cropper with an upright growth habit. Disease resistance is good. The stringless pods mature early	P/B				
CHEVRIER VERT: Once a popular haricot variety — eat as green beans, flageolet or haricot beans (see page 12)	P/B				
KINGHORN WAX: A yellow stringless bean renowned for its flavour. The pods are about 6 in. long and the flesh is creamy yellow	P/B				
MONT D'OR: Like Kinghorn Wax, a yellow 6 in. pod with a waxy texture and fine flavour. Usually cooked whole — the beans are black	P/B				
PURPLE TEEPEE: A dwarf variety which yields heavy crops. Purple pods are held above the foliage — they turn green when cooked	P/B				
BLUE LAKE: A popular climbing variety, its 5 ft stems producing a plentiful supply of white-seeded pods. Suitable for drying	P/C				
PURPLE PODDED CLIMBING: Once the most popular climbing (5 ft) variety. The round pods are fleshy and turn green when cooked	P/C				

Bush varieties: 8 lb from a 10 ft row
Climbing varieties: 12 lb from a 10 ft row

VEGETABLES A-Z

F Flat-pod variety
P Pencil-pod variety
B Bush variety
C Climbing variety

1 in. = 2.5 cm, 1 ft = 30 cm, 1 oz = 28 gm, 1 lb = 450 gm

BEAN, RUNNER

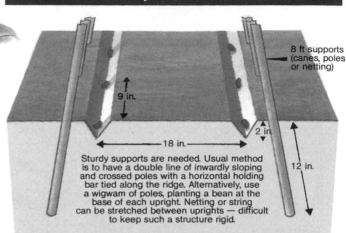

The runner bean or scarlet runner is a rewarding but not really an easy crop to grow. Thorough ground preparation is required in winter and weekly watering is necessary in dry weather once the pods have begun to form. Picking every other day is essential, but the abundance of produce makes all this work worthwhile. White-flowered varieties set more readily than the red ones.

Sturdy supports are needed. Usual method is to have a double line of inwardly sloping and crossed poles with a horizontal holding bar tied along the ridge. Alternatively, use a wigwam of poles, planting a bean at the base of each upright. Netting or string can be stretched between uprights — difficult to keep such a structure rigid.

8 ft supports (canes, poles or netting)

9 in.

18 in.

2 in.

12 in.

Tie the young plants to the supports and hoe regularly to keep down weeds. Protect from slugs and water regularly in dry weather once the pods have formed. Misting will not help fruit set but occasional liquid feeding during the cropping season will increase the yield. Pinch out growing points once the tops of the supports have been reached.

Harvesting

Pick regularly once the pods have reached a decent size (6–8 in.) but before the beans inside have started to swell. Removing all the pods at this stage will allow cropping to continue for about 8 weeks.

This means that you will have to harvest every couple of days — leaving even a small number of pods to ripen will stop production.

Types

STICK varieties (S)

Nearly all runner beans will grow 8–10 ft high and bear pods which can reach 10–20 in. long. They are grown on tall supports and the usual flower colour is red. There is a bi-colour variety (Painted Lady) and the white and pink varieties are self-pollinating.

GROUND varieties (G)

A few Stick varieties can be sown 2 ft apart and grown as bushy plants by pinching out the growing point of the main stems when they are about 12 in. high. Side shoots are pinched out and the stems are supported by short twigs. The pods appear earlier than on climbing plants but there are disadvantages. The cropping period is short and pods are often curled and soiled.

DWARF varieties (D)

True Dwarfs are available — the plants grow 12–18 in. high and the pods are 6–8 in. long. They should be grown about 6 in. apart in rows 2 ft wide. A good choice where space is limited, but yields cannot compare with their climbing relatives.

Calendar

The standard method of growing runner beans is to sow the seeds outdoors when the danger of frost is past — the end of May in the south or early June in the north. Always sow a few extra seeds at the ends of the rows — use the seedlings as transplants to fill gaps.

A second sowing in June in mild areas will ensure an October crop.

Runner beans are often raised by planting out seedlings when the danger of frost is past. These seedlings are either shop-bought (make sure that they have been properly hardened-off) or raised at home from seeds sown under glass in late April. This planting-out method is strongly recommended for the colder areas of the country.

	JAN	FEB	MAR	APR	MAY	JUN	JUL	AUG	SEP	OCT	NOV	DEC
Recommended Sowing Time (outdoors)						■						
Actual Sowing Dates (outdoors)												
Recommended Sowing Time (under glass)				▣	✿							
Actual Sowing Dates (under glass)												
Expected Picking Time								■	■	■		
Actual Picking Dates												

1 in. = 2.5 cm, 1 ft = 30 cm, 1 oz = 28 gm, 1 lb = 450 gm

For key to symbols — see page 7

Varieties

Varieties	Type	Stringless	Variety grown	Yield, flavour & notes for next year	Expected yield
PRIZEWINNER: Pods are medium length — cropping is heavy and the flavour is good. An old favourite, but the pods can be stringy	S	NO			
PRIZEWINNER STRINGLESS: One for the fans of Prizewinner. All the same features are there, but it is stringless. No longer popular	S	YES			
ENORMA: The improved form of Prizewinner — produces the slender shape and size of pod which wins prizes at the horticultural show	S	NO			
STREAMLINE: A well-established variety like Prizewinner — reliable and prolific. The problem is the stringiness of older pods	S	NO			
RED RUM: The outstanding characteristic of this variety is the ability to set seed in unsatisfactory weather conditions. Early	S	NO			
RED KNIGHT: Once in lots of catalogues, but no longer. A stringless red-flowering variety, and that is unusual. Pods are long	S	YES			
LADY DI: Dark green slender pods up to 12 in. long. Plant growth is vigorous and the flavour is excellent. There is a long cropping season	S	YES			
DESIREE: White flowers are followed by long and slender pods. Produces well even in dry weather — highly recommended	S	YES			
BUTLER: A vigorous variety which crops over a very long period. Pods are fleshy and often over 12 in. long. Hard to find	S	YES			
POLESTAR: A scarlet-flowered runner — claimed to crop very heavily. The flowers set very easily and the season starts early	S	YES			60 lb from a 10 ft double row
PAINTED LADY: Recommended as a climber to cover unsightly walls or fences — the flowers are white and red. Good for freezing	S	NO			
WHITE LADY: Like Lady Di this variety copes with bad weather better than most. You can expect high yields of fleshy pods	S	YES			
AINTREE: A recently-introduced red-flowered variety. The slim pods reach about 11 in. and the flavour is good. A heavy cropper	S	YES			
SUNSET: Different in a couple of ways — the blooms are pale pink and the self-fertilizing flowers produce a very early crop	S or G	NO			
KELVEDON MARVEL: Straight pods are produced very freely. An early cropper with rather short pods which grows well as a Ground bean	S or G	NO			
SCARLET EMPEROR: A popular choice — similar to Kelvedon Marvel in many ways. Cropping starts early etc, but pods are longer	S or G	NO			
PICKWICK: A long-established Dwarf which does not need support. Height 12 in. — crops early and for a long period if picked regularly	D	YES			
HESTIA: An excellent Dwarf for a tub or flower garden. Red and white flowers are followed by 8 in. pods. Good disease resistance	D	YES			

S Stick variety
G Ground variety
D Dwarf variety

VEGETABLES A-Z

1 in. = 2.5 cm, 1 ft = 30 cm, 1 oz = 28 gm, 1 lb = 450 gm

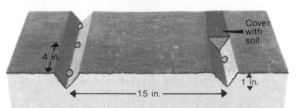

BEET, LEAF

Leaf beets are close relatives of the ordinary beetroot, but they are grown for their leaves and not the roots. Both spinach beet and swiss chard are cooked and used like spinach — with swiss chard the leaves are used as a spinach substitute and the fleshy stalks are cooked like asparagus. If your soil is sandy or infertile you should choose a leaf beet variety. Spinach grown under such conditions will either quickly run to seed or produce bitter leaves — leaf beets are much easier to grow.

Any reasonable soil in sun or light shade will do for leaf beet. Incorporate some compost or well-rotted manure during autumn digging.

Thin the seedlings to 1 ft apart when they are large enough to handle. Hoe regularly to keep the land weed-free. Bolting is most unlikely, but promptly remove any seedheads which may appear. Slugs can be a problem in late spring — spinkle Slug Pellets around the plants.

Water at fortnightly intervals during dry spells. Mulching will help to conserve moisture.

Harvesting

Twist off (do not cut) outer leaves when they are large enough for cooking — do not wait until maximum size is reached. Harvest carefully and regularly — leave the central foliage to develop for later pickings. Do not disturb the roots. Avoid storage if possible. If you must keep it, place in a polythene bag in the refrigerator for up to 2 days

Varieties

Spinach beet bears leaves which are darker, larger and fleshier than ordinary spinach. It is not a popular vegetable although the seeds appear in all the catalogues. Even less popular are the **swiss chard** varieties. They have thick and prominent midribs — the effect is attractive enough for the plant to be grown in the flower border. If the soil is heavy and low in organic matter choose a swiss chard variety rather than spinach beet.

	Type	Variety grown	Yield, flavour & notes for next year	Expected yield
SPINACH BEET: Other names — perpetual spinach, leafy beet. Contains less oxalic acid than ordinary spinach — taste is less earthy	SB			
SWISS CHARD: Other names — seakale beet, silver beet. Grows about 1½ ft high. White and fleshy midribs are 3–4 in. across	SC			
RUBY CHARD: Other name — rhubarb chard. Similar in growth habit to swiss chard but the stalks are thinner and red	SC			
RAINBOW CHARD: The leaf beet if you want something different — the stems are red, purple, yellow or white	SC			
LUCULLUS: Savoy-like leaves and broad midribs — the most prolific and hardiest of swiss chard varieties	SC			7 lb from a 10 ft row
FORDHOOK GIANT: The midribs are creamy white and exceptionally wide. In the textbooks but not in the catalogues	SC			

SB Spinach beet variety
SC Swiss chard variety

Calendar

A spring sowing will be ready for harvesting to begin in late July or early August — continue picking throughout summer and autumn. In late autumn cover the plants with cloches or straw — cropping can then continue throughout the winter months and into spring and early summer.

	JAN	FEB	MAR	APR	MAY	JUN	JUL	AUG	SEP	OCT	NOV	DEC
Recommended Sowing Time			▓	▓								
Actual Sowing Dates												
Expected Picking Time							░					
Actual Picking Dates												

1 in. = 2.5 cm, 1 ft = 30 cm, 1 oz = 28 gm, 1 lb = 450 gm

For key to symbols — see page 7

BEETROOT

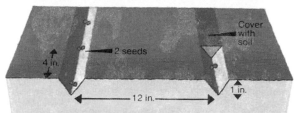

An easy vegetable which will grow in any reasonable soil. Rather slow to start, but growth is rapid once the seedlings are through. The secret is to avoid any check to growth and to pull the roots before they are large. There are 3 types — the popular globe, the less common cylindrical and the exhibitor-only long. 'Seeds' of standard varieties are corky fruits containing several true seeds. Monogerm varieties produce one seedling per seed.

When the seedlings are about 1 in. high, thin out to leave a single plant at each station. Protection against birds may be necessary. The ground must be kept weed-free.

Dryness leads to woodiness — a sudden return to wet conditions leads to splitting. To avoid problems water moderately every fortnight during dry spells.

Pull up alternate plants when roots reach golf-ball size — use for cooking. Leave the remainder to reach maturity.

Harvesting

Pull out roots of globe varieties as required. Twist off (do not cut) leaves. Roots grown for storage should be lifted in October. Shake off soil and discard damaged roots. Place the roots between layers of dry peat in a box and store in a shed. The crop will keep until March.

Varieties

Varieties	Shape & colour	Bolt ★ resistant	Variety grown	Yield, flavour & notes for next year	Expected yield
BOLTARDY: Widely available — the usual choice for early sowing. Deep red flesh		YES			
PABLO: A dark red variety with very sweet flesh. Can be grown as baby beets		YES			
MONOPOLY: A monogerm variety — noted for its flavour and resistance to woodiness		YES			
CHIOGGA: Small and sweet roots composed of red and white rings. Eat raw or cooked		NO			
CRIMSON GLOBE: Once the standard choice for later planting — but not any more		NO			
SOLO: A monogerm variety. Grow as baby beets or leave to mature		YES			Globe varieties: 10 lb from a 10 ft row / Cylindrical varieties: 14 lb from a 10 ft row / Long varieties: 18 lb from a 10 ft rcw
BURPEE'S GOLDEN: The skin is orange, and the yellow flesh does not bleed when cut		NO			
ALBINA VEREDUNA: The most popular white variety. Leaves can be cooked as greens		NO			
CYLINDRA: An oval beet with excellent keeping qualities. Deep red flesh		NO			
FORONO: Full-grown roots are an ideal size — 7 in. long and 2 in. across		NO			
CHELTENHAM GREEN TOP: An old but still highly recommended long variety		NO			
CHELTENHAM MONO: A monogerm variety — grown for showing and winter storage		YES			

★Variety which will not readily run to seed in poor growing conditions

Calendar

For a very early crop which will be ready in late May or early June, sow a bolt-resistant variety under cloches or in a frame in early March.

The main sowing period begins outdoors in mid April. A second sowing of globe varieties in mid May will provide a regular supply of tender roots.

When growing for winter storage sow in late May or June — the roots from earlier sowings may be too coarse at lifting time in October.

	JAN	FEB	MAR	APR	MAY	JUN	JUL	AUG	SEP	OCT	NOV	DEC
Recommended Sowing Time												
Actual Sowing Dates												
Expected Lifting Time												
Actual Lifting Dates												

1 in. = 2.5 cm, 1 ft = 30 cm, 1 oz = 28 gm, 1 lb = 450 gm

For key to symbols — see page 7

VEGETABLES A-Z

BROCCOLI

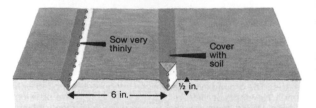

Thin seedlings to 3 in. apart in the rows. When 3 in. high transplant to permanent quarters — set seedlings 1 in. deeper than in seed bed. Leave 1½ ft between purple and white varieties — 1 ft between green varieties.

Hoe around transplants and protect from birds. Water in dry weather and apply a mulch. Watch for pests. As winter approaches draw up soil around stems and support if necessary. Netting may be needed to keep pigeons away.

The frozen spears from the supermarket are really calabrese or green broccoli — the garden grown variety is usually purple sprouting broccoli. There are four types to choose from for growing at home — all are sown in spring and planted in summer. The purple type is the hardiest and most popular — the white type is less popular and produces small cauliflower-like spears. The harvest time is February-March (early varieties) or April-May (late varieties). Green types of broccoli are cropped earlier (August-October) and should be more widely grown. Finally there is perennial broccoli which produces heads every year.

Harvesting

Cut when the spears are well formed but before the flower buds have opened. Cut or snap off the central spear first. Side shoots will appear and these should be picked regularly — never let them flower. The spears should be about 4–6 in. long and cropping lasts for about 6 weeks.

Varieties

Varieties	Colour	Variety grown	Yield, flavour & notes for next year	Expected yield
EARLY PURPLE SPROUTING: One of the more popular varieties — hardy and prolific				
RUDOLPH: Purple-sprouting type. Large spears appear from January onwards				
EARLY WHITE SPROUTING: A variety to grow for spears in March				
WHITE STAR: Small cauliflower-like heads are ready for picking in March-April				
CORVET: Large central head followed by secondary spears. Hard to find				1½ lb per plant
EXPRESS CORONA: Central head followed by secondary spears — ready in August				
GREEN DUKE: A low growing variety which starts to crop in September				
MARATHON: A calabrese type with bluish-green heads — noted for its reliability				
ROMANESCO: Pale green conical heads — both summer and winter varieties are available				
NINE STAR PERENNIAL: Produces several small cauliflower heads each year. Plant 3 ft apart				

Calendar

The date you can expect to start cutting depends on the variety and the weather. Early Purple Sprouting will be ready for its first picking in January if the winter is mild but mid spring is the peak harvesting period for the purple and white varieties.

The green varieties will be ready for cutting in autumn — choose Express Corona if you are in a hurry. Cropping will extend into winter if prolonged frosts do not occur.

	JAN	FEB	MAR	APR	MAY	JUN	JUL	AUG	SEP	OCT	NOV	DEC
Recommended Sowing Time				■	■							
Actual Sowing Dates												
Recommended Planting Time						■	■					
Actual Planting Dates												
Expected Cutting Time		EARLY vars.		LATE vars.					GREEN vars.			
Actual Cutting Dates												

For key to symbols — see page 7

BRUSSELS SPROUTS

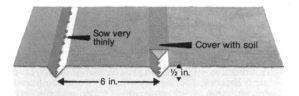

Sow very thinly — Cover with soil
½ in.
— 6 in. —

Loose, open sprouts are caused by bad gardening, not bad weather. The ground must be firm and adequately supplied with humus. Never dig or fork over the soil in spring before planting — merely tread down, rake lightly and remove surface rubbish. You can begin picking in September and finish in March if you grow both early and late varieties. These days F₁ hybrids are usually chosen — the growth habit is compact and a large number of uniform and long-lasting buttons crowd the stems. The old favourite Standard varieties have none of this uniformity nor high quality and the buttons quickly blow if not picked promptly.

Thin seedlings to 3 in. apart in the rows. When 4–6 in. high transplant to permanent quarters — set seedlings with their lowest leaves just above the soil surface. Plant firmly. Leave 1½ ft (compact F₁ hybrid varieties) — 2½ ft (Standard varieties) between plants.

Hoe around plants and protect from birds. Water in dry weather. Watch out for caterpillars and aphids — spray if necessary. As autumn approaches earth-up around the stems and stake tall varieties before the high winds of winter arrive.

Harvesting

Begin picking when the sprouts ('buttons') at the base are the size of a walnut. Tug sharply downwards or use a sharp knife. Work steadily upwards at each cropping session — remove only a few sprouts at any one time from each individual stem. Cropping lasts for about 8 weeks.

Varieties

	Type	Colour	Variety grown	Yield, flavour & notes for next year	Expected yield
PEER GYNT: Once the favourite brussels sprout, now hard to find. Early medium-sized sprouts	F₁				
BOSWORTH: A tough variety which stands up to cold winters. November-December	F₁				
WELLINGTON: Noted for its resistance to disease and frost damage. December-March	F₁				
ROGER: A good choice if you want large sprouts early in the season	F₁				
MAXIMUS: Listed in the catalogues as the replacement for Peer Gynt	F₁				
CLODIUS: Stands up well in winter — solid buttons with a good flavour. December-February	F₁				
BRILLIANT: An early variety with good disease and bolt resistance. September-October	F₁				
BRIGITTE: The one to buy if you want a sweet-flavoured sprout. Disease resistant	F₁				
TROIKA: Lacks uniformity of F₁ hybrids but gives same quality and yield	T				
BEDFORD FILLBASKET: Heavy-cropping old favourite (October-January). Sprouts are large	S				
RUBINE: The red one (October-January). Yields are low — flavour is excellent	S				2 lb per plant

F₁ F₁ hybrid variety
T Three-way cross variety
S Standard variety

Calendar

	JAN	FEB	MAR	APR	MAY	JUN	JUL	AUG	SEP	OCT	NOV	DEC
Recommended Sowing Time			▨	▨								
Actual Sowing Dates												
Recommended Planting Time				▨	▨							
Actual Planting Dates												
Expected Picking Time	▨	▨	▨						▨	▨	▨	▨
Actual Picking Dates												

Sow an early variety outdoors in mid March and plant out in mid May to provide sprouts during October and November. To obtain September sprouts, sow the seeds under cloches in early March and plant out in early May.

For a later crop which will produce sprouts between December and March, sow a late variety in April and plant out in June.

1 in. = 2.5 cm, 1 ft = 30 cm, 1 oz = 28 gm, 1 lb = 450 gm

For key to symbols — see page 7

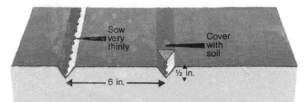

CABBAGE

If you have the space and inclination it is quite possible to have heads ready for cutting all year round. Well-consolidated soil is essential, so leave several months between digging and planting. Lime the soil if it is acid. Before planting tread down gently, rake lightly and remove surface rubbish. Nearly all of the host of varieties in the catalogues fall neatly into one of the three major groups — spring, summer or winter cabbage. The season refers to the time of harvesting, not planting. Savoys are a special type of winter cabbage — red cabbage is grown like other summer varieties.

Harvesting

Thin out spring cabbage in March and use the thinnings as spring greens. Cabbages are harvested by cutting close to ground level with a sharp knife. With spring and summer varieties cut a ½ in. deep cross into the stumps — a secondary crop of small cabbages will appear.

Thin seedlings to 3 in. apart in the rows. When there are 5 or 6 leaves transplant to permanent quarters — dip roots in Calomel Dust if club root is feared. Plant firmly. Leave 1–1½ ft between plants — 4 in. apart in 1 ft rows for spring cabbage.

Hoe around plants and protect from birds. Water in dry weather. Apply a liquid feed as the heads mature and keep watch for pests. In autumn earth-up the stems of spring cabbage.

SPRING CABBAGE

These cabbages are planted in the autumn to provide tender spring greens (collards) in early spring and larger mature heads later in the season. They are generally conical in shape and smaller than the summer and winter varieties.

	JAN	FEB	MAR	APR	MAY	JUN	JUL	AUG	SEP	OCT	NOV	DEC
Recommended Sowing Time							■	■				
Actual Sowing Dates												
Recommended Planting Time									■	■		
Actual Planting Dates												
Expected Cutting Time			■	■	■							
Actual Cutting Dates												

SUMMER CABBAGE

These cabbages are generally ball-shaped with a few conical exceptions. The normal pattern is to sow outdoors in April, transplant in May and cut in August or September. For June cabbages sow an early variety under cloches in early March.

	JAN	FEB	MAR	APR	MAY	JUN	JUL	AUG	SEP	OCT	NOV	DEC
Recommended Sowing Time		■	■	■								
Actual Sowing Dates												
Recommended Planting Time					■	■						
Actual Planting Dates												
Expected Cutting Time								■	■	■		
Actual Cutting Dates												

WINTER CABBAGE

These cabbages are generally ball-headed or drum-headed. They are green or white and suitable for immediate cooking. The white varieties are also used for Coleslaw and can be stored for months. Sow in May and transplant in July.

	JAN	FEB	MAR	APR	MAY	JUN	JUL	AUG	SEP	OCT	NOV	DEC
Recommended Sowing Time				■	■							
Actual Sowing Dates												
Recommended Planting Time						■	■					
Actual Planting Dates												
Expected Cutting Time	■	■								■	■	■
Actual Cutting Dates												

SAVOY

These cabbages are easily recognised by their crisp and puckered dark green leaves. They are grown as winter cabbages but there is a wider harvesting span — there are varieties which mature in September and others as late as March.

	JAN	FEB	MAR	APR	MAY	JUN	JUL	AUG	SEP	OCT	NOV	DEC
Recommended Sowing Time				■	■							
Actual Sowing Dates												
Recommended Planting Time							■	■				
Actual Planting Dates												
Expected Cutting Time	■	■	■						■	■	■	■
Actual Cutting Dates												

1 in. = 2.5 cm, 1 ft = 30 cm, 1 oz = 28 gm, 1 lb = 450 gm

For key to symbols — see page 7

Varieties

	Type	Variety grown	Yield, flavour & notes for next year		Expected yield
DURHAM EARLY: Popular, especially as a source of spring greens. Dark green with conical heads — forms poor quality hearts. Early	SPR				
APRIL: Another early variety which is both compact and reliable. The pointed dark green heads are rather small. Few outer leaves	SPR				
SPRING HERO: Something different — a ball-headed spring cabbage. This F_1 hybrid crops early, but sow in August and not July	SPR				
PIXIE: One of the mini-varieties which is highly recommended. Use as spring greens or leave to form firm hearts in May	SPR				
FLOWER OF SPRING: No worries about the weather with this one — it is very hardy. Large solid heads in April-May	SPR				
WHEELER'S IMPERIAL: An old variety, but still widely grown. The dark green, solid heads are small and pointed. Cut in April	SPR				
GREYHOUND: A popular variety for early sowing. The solid pointed hearts mature quickly and they are ready for cutting in July	SUM				
HISPI: This popular F_1 hybrid is even earlier than the old favourite Greyhound. Same shape, but can be cut in June	SUM				
STONEHEAD: A late summer/autumn variety with round, firm heads which will stand for a long time without splitting	SUM				
PRIMO: An old established ball-headed summer cabbage — compact and very firm. Ready in July or August — medium-sized	SUM				
MINICOLE: A popular F_1 hybrid. The small oval heads are produced in early autumn — will stand for 2-3 months without splitting	SUM				
RED DRUMHEAD: A popular red cabbage — firm and compact hearts which are dark red in colour. Can be stored until March	SUM				
CELTIC: An F_1 hybrid of a savoy and winter white cabbage. Blue-green and ball-headed — ready for cutting from November	WIN				
CHRISTMAS DRUMHEAD: Earlier than Celtic — the compact heads can be harvested in October. A reliable variety renowned for its hardiness	WIN				
JANUARY KING: Very hardy — a savoy-type but without crinkled leaves. Tinged with red — ready between November and January	WIN				
HOLLAND LATE WINTER: A white cabbage for coleslaw and storage. Heads are large and firm, and are ready in November-December	WIN				
TUNDRA: This savoy/cabbage hybrid is an outstanding popular variety. Cropping stretches from November to April. Extremely frost hardy	WIN	·			
BEST OF ALL: This one is grown for an early crop — ready in September or October. Drum-headed, solid and very large	SAV				
TARVOY: One of the new generation of savoys. Large heads of crinkled leaves mature between late autumn and early winter	SAV				

Expected yield:
Spring varieties: ¾–1 lb per plant
Summer varieties: 1½ lb per plant
Winter and savoy varieties: 2½–3 lb per plant

SPR *Spring variety*
SUM *Summer variety*
WIN *Winter variety*
SAV *Savoy variety*

1 in. = 2.5 cm, 1 ft = 30 cm, 1 oz = 28 gm, 1 lb = 450 gm

VEGETABLES A-Z

CAPSICUM

Seed Sowing

Raise seedlings under glass at 60°–70°F. Sow 2 seeds in a compost-filled peat pot — remove the weaker seedling. For pot culture it is necessary to repot in several stages until the plants are ready to be moved to their permanent site under glass. Harden off before planting outdoors.

The capsicum is a relative of the tomato and requires similar growing conditions — it is really a greenhouse crop but can be grown outdoors in the south if you are lucky with the weather. The varieties which are becoming popular are the large sweet peppers — their small and fiery relatives known as chilli peppers are much less popular. In the greenhouse the plants are grown in 9 in. pots or planted in growing bags — the stems grow about 3 ft tall. Outdoor plants are shorter — they need well-drained, fertile soil in a sunny sheltered spot. Capsicum is a difficult crop — regular watering, feeding, spraying and staking are needed.

Planting

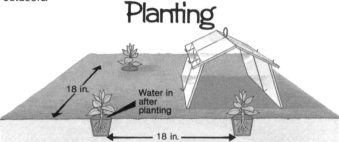

18 in.

Water in after planting

18 in.

Cover the soil with cloches for 2 weeks before planting. Replace the cloches after planting.

Mist plants regularly to keep down red spider mite and to encourage fruit set. Some form of support is necessary — attach stems to stakes or horizontal wires. Pinching out the growing point is not recommended.

Water regularly but do not keep the compost or soil sodden. Add tomato fertilizer with each watering once the fruits have begun to swell.

Harvesting

The fruits are ready for picking when the peppers are green, plump and glossy. Cut as required. You may prefer to eat them at the coloured stage rather than when they are green. You can leave them on the plant to ripen — this is practical under glass but it is usually preferable to cut the fruit and let them ripen on the windowsill when the crop is grown outdoors.

Varieties

	Colour	Variety grown	Yield, flavour & notes for next year	Expected yield
CANAPE: A popular variety — one to choose for outdoor cultivation. Prolific and early, but the fruits are rather small. Mild and sweet				
GYPSY: An F₁ hybrid recommended for cold greenhouse culture. Early, like Canape, and a heavy cropper. Slightly tapered rather than block-shaped				
LUTEUS: One of the capsicums which turn yellow when ripe. Other examples are Gold Star, Yellow Lantern and Top Banana				6–10 peppers per plant
TRITON: A compact (1 ft) variety for growing in 6 in. pots. The 4 in. fruits are highly ornamental as well as flavourful. Hard to find				
WAXLIGHTS: A mixture of fruits which turn white, red, violet or yellow when ripe. An ornamental plant, but fruits are as edible as plainer varieties				

Calendar

Prick out seedlings into 3 in. pots when 3 leaves have formed.

A straightforward greenhouse crop. Plant seedlings in pots or growing bags (3 to a bag) in late April (heated glass) or mid May (unheated glass).

A risky crop outdoors — a site against a south wall in a mild district is necessary.

	JAN	FEB	MAR	APR	MAY	JUN	JUL	AUG	SEP	OCT	NOV	DEC
Recommended Sowing & Planting Time (outdoors)			▮			✾						
Actual Sowing & Planting Dates (outdoors)												
Recommended Sowing & Planting Time (greenhouse)		▮ ▮		✾	✾							
Actual Sowing & Planting Dates (greenhouse)												
Expected Picking Time								▨	▨	▨		
Actual Picking Dates												

1 in. = 2.5 cm, 1 ft = 30 cm, 1 oz = 28 gm, 1 lb = 450 gm

For key to symbols — see page 7

CARROT

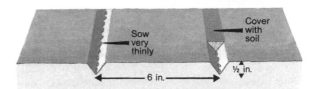

Carrots are not a difficult crop if the soil is good and the dreaded carrot fly is kept away. If your soil is stony and heavy, grow a Short-rooted variety — these carrots are golf-ball round or finger long. They are the first to be sown and mature quickly. The Intermediate-rooted varieties are the best all-rounders for the average garden. Some are pulled for immediate use and the rest are left to mature for winter storage. The Long-rooted varieties are the tapered giants of the show bench. Spectacular, but not really suitable for general garden use.

Harvesting

Pull up small carrots as required from June onwards. Ease them out with a fork if the soil is hard. October is the time to lift maincrop carrots for storage. Remove surface dirt and place between layers of sand or dry peat.

Do not add fresh manure or compost to the soil before sowing. Sow seed very thinly to reduce the need for thinning to a minimum. Thin seedlings to 2–3 in. apart when they are large enough to handle. Protect against carrot fly by thinning in the evening and burning or burying the removed seedlings.

Pull out weeds by hand — avoid hoeing if possible. Water during periods of drought in order to keep the ground moist — a downpour on dry soil may cause root splitting.

Varieties

	Type	Shape	Variety grown	Yield, flavour & notes for next year	Expected yield
AMSTERDAM FORCING: One of the earliest — needs little care and excellent for freezing	S				
EARLY NANTES: Like Amsterdam Forcing — early, tender and good for freezing	S				
PARMEX: The most popular round carrot — 1-2 in. across. Suitable for tubs and growbags	S				
CHAMPION SCARLET HORN: An early variety recommended for sowing under cloches	S				
PARIS MARKET: A good carrot for bad soils or small plots. Almost ball-shaped	S				
CHANTENEY RED CORED: An old favourite — smooth-skinned and deep orange	I				
AUTUMN KING: Unusually long for an Intermediate. Extremely hardy and healthy	I				
FLYAWAY: Good resistance to carrot fly attack is its main claim to fame	I				
JAMES SCARLET INTERMEDIATE: An old favourite renowned for all-round performance	I				
SUPERSNAX: An early variety which can be grown for mini-carrot production. Bolt resistant	I				
NEW RED INTERMEDIATE: Despite the name, one of the longest of all carrots	L				
ST VALERY: Long and finely tapered — a popular choice for exhibition	L				
					Early carrots: 8 lb from a 10 ft row / Maincrop carrots: 10 lb from a 10 ft row

S Short-rooted variety
I Intermediate-rooted variety
L Long-rooted variety

Calendar

		JAN	FEB	MAR	APR	MAY	JUN	JUL	AUG	SEP	OCT	NOV	DEC
For a very early crop which will be ready in June, sow a Short-rooted variety under cloches or in a cold frame in early March.	**Recommended Sowing Time**												
For an early crop which will be ready in July, sow a Short-rooted variety in a sheltered spot in late March or early April.	**Actual Sowing Dates**												
For maincrop carrots sow Intermediate- or Long-rooted varieties between mid April and early June for lifting in September and October.	**Expected Lifting Time**												
For a tender crop in November and December, sow a Short-rooted variety in August and cover with cloches from October.	**Actual Lifting Dates**												

1 in. = 2.5 cm, 1 ft = 30 cm, 1 oz = 28 gm, 1 lb = 450 gm

For key to symbols — see page 7

CAULIFLOWER

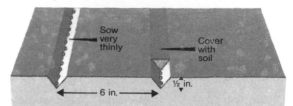

Cauliflower is more difficult to grow than cabbage. It needs deep and rich soil which must be well-consolidated — never dig in spring prior to planting. You must make sure there is no check to growth, which calls for regular watering in dry weather. Failure to provide the right conditions will result in the production of tiny 'button' heads. Varieties are available to produce heads nearly all year round, but avoid the Roscoff types which are not hardy in most parts of the country. You can grow a giant, such as Flora Blanca, or a compact type like Alpha-Polaris.

Harvesting

Do not wait for all the heads to mature — cut some while they are still quite small. Harvest in the morning when the heads still have dew on them — in frosty weather wait until midday. Cut all cauliflowers before the florets start to separate.

Thin seedlings to 3 in. apart in the rows. When there are 5 or 6 leaves transplant to permanent quarters — add lime to the soil before planting to reduce the risk of club root. Plant firmly. Leave 2 ft between summer and autumn varieties, 2½ ft between winter varieties.

Hoe around plants and protect from birds. Water in dry weather and feed occasionally. With summer types bend a few leaves over the curd to protect it from the sun — with winter types a few leaves broken over the curd will protect the head from frost and snow.

Types

SUMMER CAULIFLOWER

These cauliflowers mature during the summer months from seed sown in a cold frame in September, in a greenhouse or on the windowsill in January or outdoors in April. They are compact plants — you can choose an early variety, such as Snowball, which will produce heads in June or July, or you can grow a later-maturing type like All the Year Round which will be ready for cutting in August from an outdoor sowing.

AUTUMN CAULIFLOWER

These cauliflowers mature during the autumn months and are of two quite different types. There are the large and vigorous varieties such as Autumn Giant and Flora Blanca, and there are the more compact Australian varieties such as Canberra.

WINTER CAULIFLOWER

'Winter cauliflower' is the technically incorrect name for the group of varieties listed on the next page. The standard types mature in spring, not winter, and they are really heading broccoli. Although less delicately-flavoured than true cauliflowers the popular varieties of winter cauliflower are easier to grow.

Calendar

Summer varieties: In late March or early April transplant seedlings which have been raised under glass from a January sowing to provide a June-July crop. Or sow outdoors in early April and transplant in June for cropping in August-September.

Autumn varieties: Sow outdoors between mid April and mid May and transplant in late June.

Winter varieties: Sow outdoors in May and transplant in late July.

	JAN	FEB	MAR	APR	MAY	JUN	JUL	AUG	SEP	OCT	NOV	DEC
Recommended Sowing Time			░	░	░							
Actual Sowing Dates												
Recommended Planting Time						░	░					
Actual Planting Dates												
Expected Cutting Time			WINTER vars.				SUMMER vars.			AUTUMN vars.		
Actual Cutting Dates												

1 in. = 2.5 cm, 1 ft = 30 cm, 1 oz = 28 gm, 1 lb = 450 gm

For key to symbols — see page 7

Variety

Varieties

Varieties	Type	Variety grown	Yield, flavour & notes for next year	Expected yield
ALL THE YEAR ROUND: For many years the No. 1 choice, but not now. White, large curds which are excellent for cooking, freezing and exhibiting	SUM			
IGLOO: The seedlings are set close together at planting time to produce mini-caulis, or are left to mature for an early midsummer crop	SUM			
NAUTILUS: A variety which tolerates poorer conditions than most other types. The curd is well protected by the leaves and the flavour is good	SUM			
SNOWBALL: An early cauliflower which is no longer popular. The heads are tight but not large. For large heads choose the F₁ hybrid Snow Crown	SUM			
WHITE ROCK: A reliable variety — sow in succession for late summer to early autumn heads. The curds are well protected by the foliage	SUM			
VIOLET QUEEN: Mauve heads which are attractive when served raw as crudité — turns green when cooked. Cutting can start in August	AUT			
TREVI: Pale green heads which keep their colour when cooked. Medium size. Sow in May for September crop. Good flavour	AUT			
WALLABY: An Australian variety which is noted for its unusually large heads. The cutting season is in September-March — good for freezing	AUT			
AUTUMN GIANT: The dominant autumn type before the Australian varieties appeared. Still useful if you want large heads in early winter	AUT			
FLORA BLANCA: Another old favourite — once a popular choice for exhibition. The extra-large heads are ready in September-October	AUT			
GRAFFITI: One of the coloured cauliflowers — this one is the deepest purple. Leave the curd uncovered — cutting can start in August	AUT			
LATEMAN: A vigorous cauliflower which produces medium-sized heads. Use the leaves to protect the curds — cut in August-November	AUT			
CANBERRA: One of the early Australian varieties which matures in November. The curd is well protected by the broad leaves	AUT			
CHEDDAR: One for the novelty-plant lover. Orange heads for cutting in late summer or autumn — leave the curd exposed during growth	AUT			
WALCHEREN WINTER: A Dutch variety which took over from English Winter. Heads are claimed to be superior in quality	WIN			
PURPLE CAPE: Purple heads instead of the usual white. Large and hardy — ready for cutting in March. Cook leaves as well as curd	WIN			
GALLEON: An overwintering type which produces large heads — the leaves provide good protection for the curd. Cut in April	WIN			
JEROME: Another overwintering type which stands up well to the frost and snow. The heads are ready for cutting in early spring	WIN			

Expected yield: Summer varieties: ½–1 lb per plant; Autumn varieties: 1–2 lb per plant; Winter varieties: ½–1 lb per plant

VEGETABLES A-Z

SUM *Summer variety*
AUT *Autumn variety*
WIN *Winter variety*

1 in. = 2.5 cm, 1 ft = 30 cm, 1 oz = 28 gm, 1 lb = 450 gm

CELERIAC

Seed Sowing

Sow two seeds in a compost-filled pot — remove the weakest seedling. Harden off the seedlings before planting outdoors.

Planting

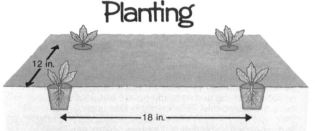

12 in.

18 in.

A popular vegetable in parts of Europe but it is not often seen in British shops or allotments. The knobbly, swollen stem-bases known as 'roots' are about 4-5 in. across and are peeled, cubed and boiled like turnips. The flavour is distinctly celery-like, hence the common name 'turnip-rooted celery'. This is not a vegetable for all gardens. Try some before deciding to grow it as the flavour does not appeal to everyone. It is also not an easy plant to grow — rich, moisture-retentive soil is required and so is regular watering. Slugs, carrot fly and celery fly can be a nuisance.

Plant firmly with the stem-base at ground level. Do not bury the crown. Water in after planting.

Hoe regularly and feed occasionally. Water thoroughly if dry spells occur during the growing season — a mulch in early summer will help to conserve moisture.

Remove side shoots — from midsummer onwards cut off the lower leaves so as to expose the crown. In late September draw soil around the swollen stem-bases.

Harvesting

There is no point in lifting the roots before they reach maximum size — neither flavour nor texture deteriorate with age. Lifting begins in October — use a garden fork. In most areas there is no need to store the roots — just cover the plants with straw or fleece and lift as required until spring. In heavy soils lift all roots in November and store in damp sand.

Varieties

	Variety grown	Yield, flavour & notes for next year	Expected yield
MARBLE BALL: Once the best-known variety but now found in few catalogues. Medium-sized and strongly flavoured			7 lb from a 10 ft row
MONARCH: The king of the celeriac world. Smooth skin, tender flesh, virus tolerant. Autumn-early winter			
PRINZ: Not popular like Monarch, but it has its points. Large roots, early and slow to bolt			
BRILLIANT: Has a place in the catalogues because of its exceptional flavour and it keeps well in store			
TELLUS: Quick-growing with a smoother skin than most varieties. Flesh remains white when cooked			
GIANT PRAGUE: This variety is noted for the large size of the roots. Flavour is stronger than average			
SNOW WHITE: An early celeriac with the whitest flesh of all. Roots are large and round			
GLOBUS: Matures rather late, but the weight is larger than average and the roots store well			

Calendar

Celeriac is not hardy — seedlings have to be raised from seeds sown under glass in early spring.

Seedlings are planted in their permanent site outdoors when all danger of frost is past.

	JAN	FEB	MAR	APR	MAY	JUN	JUL	AUG	SEP	OCT	NOV	DEC
Recommended Sowing Time			■■									
Actual Sowing Dates												
Recommended Planting Time					🌱	🌱						
Actual Planting Dates												
Expected Lifting Time												
Actual Lifting Dates												

1 in. = 2.5 cm, 1 ft = 30 cm, 1 oz = 28 gm, 1 lb = 450 gm

For key to symbols — see page 7

CELERY

Seed Sowing

Sow seeds under glass. Prepare the trench in April. Seedlings are ready for transplanting when there are 5-6 leaves — harden off before planting outdoors.

The Trench varieties involve a lot of effort — the planting site must be carefully prepared and the crop must be earthed-up at intervals to lengthen and remove the stringiness from the stems. Nowadays there are Self-blanching varieties to make the task of celery growing easier. Trenching and earthing-up are not necessary, but there are drawbacks. The flavour is less pronounced and the crop cannot be left in the ground once the frosts arrive. Furthermore Self-blanching celery is not an 'easy' crop — regular watering and feeding and humus-rich soil are still required.

Planting

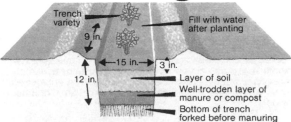

Trench variety — 9 in. — 15 in. — 3 in. — 12 in. — Fill with water after planting — Layer of soil — Well-trodden layer of manure or compost — Bottom of trench forked before manuring

Plant Self-blanching varieties 9 in. apart in a block, not in rows. Water copiously and feed regularly during the summer months.

Begin blanching Trench varieties in early August by covering stems with newspaper or cardboard and then filling the trench with soil. In late August mound moist soil against the stems. In September heap up again so that only the green tops are showing. Do not let soil fall into the hearts.

Harvesting

Lift white Trenching varieties from October to Christmas — pink and red ones in January. Start at one end of the row — replace soil to protect remaining plants. Lift Self-blanching varieties as required from August until the frosts arrive. Do not pull — use a trowel to avoid disturbing neighbouring plants.

Varieties

	Type	Colour	Variety grown	Yield, flavour & notes for next year	Expected yield
GIANT WHITE: The standard white-stalked celery — needs good growing conditions. Various strains (e.g Solid White) are sold	T				
GIANT PINK: Similar to Giant White, but sticks are tinged with pink. Hardy — ready for lifting in late winter	T				
GIANT RED: Very hardy variety — the sticks are greenish purple, turning pink when blanched. Heads are large and firm	T				
GOLDEN SELF-BLANCHING: The standard yellow-stalked celery — low-growing and ready for lifting from August onwards	SB				12 lb from a 10 ft row
LATHOM SELF-BLANCHING: An alternative to Golden Self-Blanching if you want a yellow variety — less likely to bolt	SB				
CELEBRITY: Similar to Lathom Self-Blanching in earliness and bolt-resistance, but the sticks are longer	SB				
VICTORIA: The most popular self-blanching variety. Easy to grow — the apple-green stalks are crisp and store well	SB				

T Trench variety
SB Self-blanching variety

Calendar

Buy celery seedlings for planting in late May-mid June. Or raise your own by sowing seed under heated glass between mid March and early April — make sure that the seedlings do not receive any check to growth and ensure that the plants are properly hardened off before planting.

Self-blanching varieties will be ready for lifting between August and October. The Trench varieties are grown for winter use from October onwards.

	JAN	FEB	MAR	APR	MAY	JUN	JUL	AUG	SEP	OCT	NOV	DEC
Recommended Sowing Time			▓	▓								
Actual Sowing Dates												
Recommended Planting Time					🌱	🌱						
Actual Planting Dates												
Expected Lifting Time	▓	▒						▒	▓	▓	▓	▓
Actual Lifting Dates												

1 in. = 2.5 cm, 1 ft = 30 cm, 1 oz = 28 gm, 1 lb = 450 gm

For key to symbols — see page 7

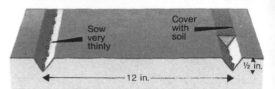

CHICORY

There are two basic types. The Forcing chicories are the more popular, producing plump leafy heads ('chicons') from roots kept in the dark during the winter months. The usual colour is white, but red ones can be forced to produce the red and white leaves served as *radicchio*. The other chicories are the Non-forcing varieties which do not require blanching — they produce large lettuce-like heads which are ready in autumn. Chicons have never become really popular in the U.K. Bitterness is the problem — remember that home-grown ones kept in the dark are much less bitter than shop-bought chicons.

Choose a sunny site. Thin the seedlings to 6 in. (Forcing varieties) or 12 in. (Non-forcing varieties). Hoe to keep down weeds — water in dry weather.

Lift the parsnip-like roots of Forcing chicory in November — discard ones with crowns less than 1 in. across. Cut roots to 6 in. and leaves to 1 in. above the crown — store horizontally in sand. To produce chicons plant 5 roots in a 9 in. pot of peat in November–March. Leave crowns exposed. Cover pot with an empty larger one — block the drainage hole. Keep at 50°–60°F.

Harvesting

Cut chicons after 3–4 weeks forcing — they should be about 6 in. high. Cut just above the crown and then water the compost. Replace the cover — small secondary chicons will be produced. Cut Non-forcing chicory in autumn — use immediately or store in a cool shed.

Varieties

	Type	Variety grown	Yield, flavour & notes for next year	Expected yield
WITLOOF: Belgian Chicory — the traditional Forcing variety. Needs a soil covering rather than an upturned pot	F			
NORMATO: A modern Forcing variety which produces firm chicons. Easier to grow than Witloof	F			
ZOOM: An F₁ hybrid Forcing variety which produces compact chicons. Easier to grow than Witloof	F			
SUGAR LOAF: The traditional Non-forcing variety. Matures in October — looks rather like a Cos lettuce	NF			
PALLA ROSSA: The leaves are red with white veins — a typical radicchio. Colour deepens as winter approaches	NF			
ROSSA DE VERONA: A red chicory which has a round cluster of leaves — cabbage-like in appearance	NF			
TREVISO: An upright red-leaved chicory. Treat as a Forcing or Non-forcing variety	F or NF			

F Forcing variety
NF Non-forcing variety

Calendar

		JAN	FEB	MAR	APR	MAY	JUN	JUL	AUG	SEP	OCT	NOV	DEC
FORCING varieties	Recommended Sowing Time					■							
	Actual Sowing Dates												
	Expected Cutting Time	■	■	■	■								■
	Actual Cutting Dates												
NON-FORCING varieties	Recommended Sowing Time						■	■					
	Actual Sowing Dates												
	Expected Cutting Time										■	■	
	Actual Cutting Dates												

1 in. = 2.5 cm, 1 ft = 30 cm, 1 oz = 28 gm, 1 lb = 450 gm

For key to symbols — see page 7

COURGETTE

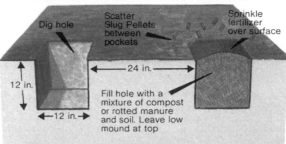

Courgettes are nothing more than marrows cut at an immature stage. The flesh is firmer and the taste superior — in recent years they have taken over from the large watery vegetable marrows. Courgettes are now plentiful in the shops and bountiful in the garden where scores can be obtained from just a few plants. Choose a compact bush variety which is recommended for courgette rather than marrow production. It is essential that you cut all the fruits at the small courgette stage — if you let just a few mature into marrows then production will cease. Blanch for about 2 minutes in boiling water to remove bitterness before serving raw in salads.

Sow 3 seeds 1 in. deep at the centre of each pocket — cover with a cloche. Remove the 2 weaker seedlings. Plants can be raised indoors, but this method is often less satisfactory. Place a single seed edgeways ½ in. deep in compost — keep at minimum 65°F.

Water copiously around the plants in dry weather — place black polythene or a mulch under the stems before fruit formation. Once the fruits start to swell feed regularly with a liquid fertilizer.

Harvesting

Remove the fruits when they are still quite small — 4–5 in. is the ideal size. Do not pull them off the stems — use a sharp knife. Continual cropping is essential.

Varieties

	Type	Colour	Variety grown	Yield, flavour & notes for next year	Expected yield
ZUCCHINI: Once the most popular courgette variety — dark green fruits borne in profusion. Serve raw or cook as a hot vegetable	S				
ORELIA: There are not many golden varieties on offer — this one is a true yellow. Heavy cropper — 6 in. fruits	F₁				
GOLD RUSH: The golden-yellow fruits are narrow — the flesh is creamy-white with a good flavour. Compact plants	F₁				
GREEN BUSH: One of the favourite all-rounders — cut the small fruits as courgettes and let a few mature into large, striped marrows	F₁				16 courgettes per plant
DEFENDER: The popular choice — you will find it in many catalogues. Very high yields — good virus resistance	F₁				
AMBASSADOR: This variety is claimed to be very high yielding over a long season. Open growth habit makes picking easier	F₁				
VENUS: Compact growth habit makes this one suitable for small gardens. Early cropper — good for the show bench	F₁				

S Standard variety
F₁ F₁ hybrid variety

Calendar

Sow outdoors in late May or early June. In the Midlands and northern areas cover the seedlings with cloches if you can for a few weeks. The first courgettes will be ready in July.

For an earlier crop sow seeds under glass in late April. Plant out the seedlings in early June when the danger of frost has passed.

	JAN	FEB	MAR	APR	MAY	JUN	JUL	AUG	SEP	OCT	NOV	DEC
Recommended Sowing Time (outdoors)						●						
Actual Sowing Dates (outdoors)												
Recommended Sowing Time (under glass)				●	●							
Actual Sowing Dates (under glass)												
Expected Cutting Time								●	●			
Actual Cutting Dates												

1 in. = 2.5 cm, 1 ft = 30 cm, 1 oz = 28 gm, 1 lb = 450 gm

For key to symbols — see page 7

CUCUMBER, GREENHOUSE

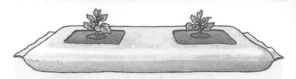

If you want fruits in May or June then growing cucumbers under glass rather than outdoors is necessary. A well-grown specimen of a greenhouse (or frame) cucumber is straight, cylindrical, smooth-skinned and shiny. But it is also a difficult thing to grow. Warmth, high humidity, regular watering and feeding, pest control, regular stopping and so on are all required. Ordinary varieties are the traditional type — long and straight, but male flowers have to be removed or fruit will be bitter. All-female varieties are available.

Sow seed edgeways ½ in. deep in a 3 in. pot. Plant out 1 per pot, 2 per growing bag.

Maintain minimum of 60°F (Ordinary varieties) or 70°F (All-female varieties). Keep compost and air moist — spray floor to maintain high humidity.

Train stems up a wire or cane. Pinch out the tip of each side shoot at 2 leaves beyond a female (swollen base) flower. Remove all male flowers. Feed every 2 weeks once fruits have started to swell.

Harvesting

Cut (do not pull) when the fruit has reached a reasonable size and the sides are parallel. Cropping will cease if you allow cucumbers to mature and turn yellow on the plant.

Varieties

	Type	Variety grown	Yield, flavour & notes for next year	Expected yield
TELEGRAPH: Still the most popular Ordinary variety, but not in many catalogues	O			25 cucumbers per plant
CONQUEROR: Once a popular choice for growing under cool conditions, now hard to find	O			
CARMEN: A popular variety. Abundant yields, but length is average. Good disease resistance	F			
CUCINO: Prolific crop of mini-cues. Good choice for a cold house. Good flavour	F			
PETITA: Small fruits, about 8 in. long, borne in large numbers. Easy to grow	F			
PASSANDRA: Another mini-cue variety. Key features here are early cropping and high yields	F			
PALERMO: Long, dark green fruits — good tolerance to powdery mildew. Suitable for a cold house	F			
FEMBABY: One for the windowsill — compact plants, small fruits and easy to train. Not easy to find	F			
SALADIN: Some of the varieties here produce mini-cues — this one can provide fruits over 1 ft long	F			
FEMSPOT: For heated houses only — long, bitter-free fruits appear early. Not easy to find	F			
TIFFANY: Like Saladin, a variety to choose if you want foot-long fruits. Suitable for a cold house	F			

O Ordinary variety
F All-female variety

Calendar

Sowing should take place in late February or early March for planting in a heated greenhouse or late April for an unheated greenhouse or frame.

Plant out in late March (heated greenhouse) or late May (unheated greenhouse).

	JAN	FEB	MAR	APR	MAY	JUN	JUL	AUG	SEP	OCT	NOV	DEC
Recommended Sowing Time		■	■ ▨	▨ ■	▨							
Actual Sowing Dates												
Expected Cutting Time												
Actual Cutting Dates												

1 in. = 2.5 cm, 1 ft = 30 cm, 1 oz = 28 gm, 1 lb = 450 gm

For key to symbols — see page 7

CUCUMBER, OUTDOOR

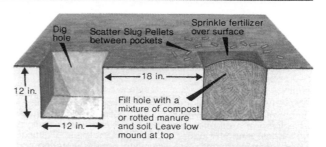

Dig hole

Scatter Slug Pellets between pockets

Sprinkle fertilizer over surface

12 in.

18 in.

12 in.

Fill hole with a mixture of compost or rotted manure and soil. Leave low mound at top

Outdoor (or ridge) cucumbers have developed remarkably since the 1970s. The Standard ridge varieties do still exist — short, dumpy fruits with warty skins. So do the Gherkin varieties which are even smaller and equally knobbly, but now there are the All-female varieties which are almost seed-free and also the Japanese varieties which are long, smooth and straight like greenhouse cucumbers. Finally there is the small Ball group with round and yellow fruits.

See page 30 for details of seed sowing — keep seeds under glass at 70°–80°F until germinated. Pinch out growing tips when stems have 6–7 leaves — train up netting or leave to trail. Remove non-flowering shoots at the 7th leaf.

Water around plants and mist in dry weather. Place black polythene over the soil before fruit formation. Do not remove male flowers. Feed once the first fruits have started to swell.

Harvesting

Cut before the fruits reach maximum size in order to encourage further fruiting. Most types will be 6-8 in. long. Use a sharp knife — don't tug them. The harvesting period is quite short — the plants are killed by the first frosts.

Varieties

	Type	Variety grown	Yield, flavour & notes for next year	Expected yield
CHINESE LONG GREEN: The fruits are smooth-skinned and about 1 ft long	S			10 cucumbers per plant
TOKYO SLICER: A Japanese variety — slender and smooth-skinned like a supermarket cucumber	S			
KYOTO: Another Japanese type — now hard to find in the catalogues	S			
BURPLESS TASTY GREEN: A good one to choose — short fruits devoid of bitterness	S			
MARKETMORE: Does better than most in poor conditions. Good resistance to virus and mildews	S			
MASTERPIECE: The straight 8 in. fruits are slightly spiny — grow as a climber	S			
LONG WHITE: Something different. The short fruits have pale creamy skin — no need to peel	S			
SWING: An all-female variety which provides a heavy crop of 8 in. dark green fruits	S			
VENLO PICKLING: The most popular Gherkin grown for pickling. Small and warty	G			
CRYSTAL APPLE: Yellow and apple-like — replaced by Crystal Lemon in the catalogues	B			
CRYSTAL LEMON: Nothing like a cucumber — pale yellow, round fruits for eating fresh or pickling	B			

S Standard variety   **G** Gherkin variety   **B** Ball variety

Calendar

Sow outdoors in late May or early June. In the Midlands and northern areas cover the seedlings with cloches if you can for a few weeks. Cropping should start in early August.

For an earlier crop sow seeds under glass in late April. Plant out the seedlings in early June when the danger of frost has passed.

	JAN	FEB	MAR	APR	MAY	JUN	JUL	AUG	SEP	OCT	NOV	DEC
Recommended Sowing Time (outdoors)					▓							
Actual Sowing Dates (outdoors)												
Recommended Sowing Time (under glass)				▣		🌱						
Actual Sowing Dates (under glass)												
Expected Cutting Time								▓	▓			
Actual Cutting Dates												

1 in. = 2.5 cm, 1 ft = 30 cm, 1 oz = 28 gm, 1 lb = 450 gm

For key to symbols — see page 7

KALE

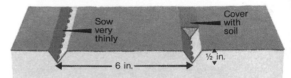

The books sing the praises of kale (or borecole) as a source of winter and spring greens, but gardeners take little notice. It is the hardiest of all vegetables, grows in poor soil and is untroubled by all the dreaded brassica pests. The problem is the bitter taste, but that is avoidable these days. Choose a modern variety, pick the leaves when they are young and tender, and cook them properly. Curly kales are the popular ones, the Plain-leaved varieties are cropped in early spring and Rape kale is harvested in March-May. Best of all is the Leaf & spear variety.

Sow very thinly — Cover with soil — 6 in. — ½ in.

Thin seedlings to 3 in. apart — transplant when they are 4-6 in. high. Plant firmly, with the lowest leaves just above the soil surface. Leave 18 in. between the plants.

Treat Rape kale varieties differently. Sow where the plants will grow — leave 18 in. between the rows and 18 in. between the plants.

Hoe regularly, firm the plants if necessary and water in dry weather. Earth-up around the stems as autumn approaches — stake tall varieties.

Harvesting

Pick your leaves from the crown of Curly kale varieties from November onwards. In spring gather side shoots when they are 4-5 in. long. Break off or use a sharp knife.

Varieties

	Type		Variety grown	Yield, flavour & notes for next year	Expected yield
DWARF GREEN CURLED: The most popular variety, especially for a small plot. The 1½-2 ft plants do not need staking and the flavour is good	CL				
REDBOR: The most popular Curly-leaved type. Tall, attractive enough for the flower garden. Use young growth in salads	CL				
RED RUSSIAN: Green leaves with purple veins. Noted for its tenderness — use young leaves to add colour to salads	CL				
AFRO: A mid-green kale with two key features. It is a compact modern variety and the yields are above average	CL				2 lb per plant
THOUSAND-HEADED KALE: Sometimes praised in the textbooks. It is very hardy and prolific, but you would do better with Pentland Brig	PL				
BLACK TUSCANY: You will find this dark green kale in many catalogues. Knobbly, strap-like leaves. Pick tender young growth	PL				
HUNGRY GAP: A late cropper, like all Rape kales. Robust and reliable, producing shoots which are suitable for freezing	RK				
PENTLAND BRIG: Pick young leaves in November, young shoots in early spring and broccoli-like spears in mid spring. Obviously a good choice	LS				

CL Curly-leaved variety   **RK** Rape kale variety
PL Plain-leaved variety   **LS** Leaf & spear variety

Calendar

If you want greens before Christmas, sow a variety of Curly-leaved kale in April. For later cropping sow Leaf & spear or Plain-leaved kale in May. The correct time for transplanting is governed by the height of the seedlings rather than the date.

Thin in stages to leave 18 in. between the plants.

Rape kale is sown in late June. For later management of the crop see details above.

	JAN	FEB	MAR	APR	MAY	JUN	JUL	AUG	SEP	OCT	NOV	DEC
Recommended Sowing Time												
Actual Sowing Dates												
Recommended Planting Time												
Actual Planting Dates												
Expected Cutting Time												
Actual Cutting Dates												

1 in. = 2.5 cm, 1 ft = 30 cm, 1 oz = 28 gm, 1 lb = 450 gm

For key to symbols — see page 7

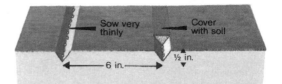

LEEK

VEGETABLES A-Z

Leeks are less demanding than onions and will grow in any reasonable soil. They will withstand the hardest winter, are generally untroubled by pests and diseases and do not demand a high level of fertility. Still, they are not an 'easy' crop — transplanting and earthing-up are required and the land is occupied for a long time. The Early varieties are sown under glass for a September crop or outdoors for an autumn harvest. The Mid-season varieties are the most popular ones with a harvest period from December to January. The Late varieties mature between February and April.

Harvesting

Begin lifting when the leeks are quite small — flavour decreases as size increases. Do not pull the plants out of the ground — use a fork. Lift during the winter as required.

Thin seedlings to 1½ in. apart — transplant when they are 8 in. high and as thick as a pencil. Trim off root ends and leaf tips, then set out 6 in. apart in rows 12 in. apart. Use a dibber — drop plant into a 6 in. deep hole and fill with water to settle roots.

Hoe and water as necessary. Earth-up during the season, drawing up soil around the stems at intervals so as to increase the length of white stem. Do not let soil fall between leaves. Finish in late October.

Varieties

Varieties	Type	Variety grown	Yield, flavour & notes for next year	Expected yield
LYON-PRIZETAKER: A favourite exhibition variety over the years. Mild flavoured and long-stemmed	E			
PANCHO: A modern Early — long, straight stems which can stand until mid winter. Does not need blanching	E			
JULANT: A long-shafted very Early variety. Root resistant. Grow for mini-leeks	E			
MUSSELBURGH: The favourite home-grown leek — hardy, reliable and thick-stemmed	M			
OARSMAN: A dark-leaved leek which shows good resistance to bolting and rust	M			
APOLLO: A high-yielding variety for lifting from December onwards. Rust-resistant	M			
KING RICHARD: The stems are significantly longer than most other Mid-season varieties. Grow for mini-leeks	M			
TOLEDO: The straight, smooth shafts are longer than average. Dark foliage. Rust-resistant	L			10 lb from a 10 ft row

E Early variety
M Mid-season variety
L Late variety

Calendar

For exhibiting in the autumn sow seed under glass in late January or February and plant outdoors during April.

For ordinary kitchen use sow seed outdoors in spring when the soil is workable and warm enough to permit germination — for all but warm and sheltered areas this means mid March or later. Transplant the seedlings in June.

For an April crop you can sow seed of a Late variety in June and transplant in July.

	JAN	FEB	MAR	APR	MAY	JUN	JUL	AUG	SEP	OCT	NOV	DEC
Recommended Sowing Time												
Actual Sowing Dates												
Recommended Planting Time												
Actual Planting Dates												
Expected Lifting Time												
Actual Lifting Dates												

1 in. = 2.5 cm, 1 ft = 30 cm, 1 oz = 28 gm, 1 lb = 450 gm

For key to symbols — see page 7

LETTUCE

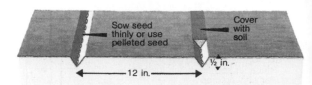

Lettuce is grown everywhere. A row or two is sown in spring and again in early summer, the seedlings are thinned and the heads are cut when a heart has formed. The results are often disappointing — plants quickly bolt, leaves are leathery or there is a glut and famine situation. The answer is to sow very short rows every two weeks and to follow the rules — lime if necessary, thin as soon as possible, don't transplant, and water regularly. The cabbage types (Butterhead and Crisphead varieties) dominate the catalogues, but both Cos and Loose-leaf varieties are worth growing.

Labels in diagram: Sow seed thinly or use pelleted seed — Cover with soil — 12 in. — ½ in.

Thin seedlings as soon as the first true leaves appear. Continue thinning until the plants are 12 in. apart – 9 in. for Tom Thumb and Little Gem.

You can try transplanting but lettuce hates to be moved. Wherever possible sow seed where the plants are to mature. Protect seedlings from slugs and birds. Hoe as required.

Water in the morning in dry weather — never in the evening. Keep watch for greenfly and grey mould.

Harvesting

Lettuce is ready for cutting as soon as a firm heart has formed — leaving it will result in the heart growing upwards (bolting). Pull up the whole plant and cut off the root and lower leaves.

Types

LOOSE-LEAF varieties

These varieties do not produce a heart. The leaves are curled and are picked like spinach — a few at a time without cutting the whole plant. Sow seed in April or May.

COS varieties

The Cos or Romaine lettuce is easy to recognise by its upright growth habit and oblong head. The leaves are crisp and the flavour is good. They are generally a little more difficult to grow than the cabbage types and take longer to mature.

CRISPHEAD varieties

The Crispheads produce large hearts of curled and crisp leaves. In general they are more resistant to bolting than Butterheads, and their popularity has increased in Britain. They have always been the popular group in the U.S. where the Iceberg type (Crispheads with a solid heart and few outer leaves) are dominant.

BUTTERHEAD varieties

The Butterheads are still the most popular lettuce group. They are quick-maturing and will generally tolerate poorer conditions than the other types. The leaves are soft and smooth-edged — most are summer varieties but a few are hardy lettuces which are used to produce a spring crop and several others are forcing varieties for growing under glass.

Calendar

For a Summer/Autumn Crop

Sow outdoors in late March-late July for cutting in June-October. For an earlier crop (mid May-early June) sow under glass in early February and plant out in early March under cloches.

	JAN	FEB	MAR	APR	MAY	JUN	JUL	AUG	SEP	OCT	NOV	DEC
Recommended Sowing Time		▣	✿	▩	▩	▩	▩					
Actual Sowing Dates												
Expected Cutting Time						▩	▩	▩	▩	▩		
Actual Cutting Dates												

For an Early Winter Crop

Sow a mildew-resistant variety such as Clarion outdoors in early August. Cover with cloches in late September — close ends with panes of glass. The crop will be ready for cutting in November or December.

	JAN	FEB	MAR	APR	MAY	JUN	JUL	AUG	SEP	OCT	NOV	DEC
Recommended Sowing Time								▩				
Actual Sowing Dates												
Expected Cutting Time											▩	▩
Actual Cutting Dates												

For a Spring Crop

If you live in a mild part of the country, sow a winter-hardy variety such as Valdor or Winter Density outdoors in late August-early September. Thin to 3 in. apart in October — complete thinning to 12 in. spacing in early spring. The crop will be ready in May. For less favoured areas sow in mid October under cloches — harvest in April. Use a winter-hardy or a forcing variety.

	JAN	FEB	MAR	APR	MAY	JUN	JUL	AUG	SEP	OCT	NOV	DEC
Recommended Sowing Time								▩	▩	▩		
Actual Sowing Dates												
Expected Cutting Time				▩	▩							
Actual Cutting Dates												

1 in. = 2.5 cm, 1 ft = 30 cm, 1 oz = 28 gm, 1 lb = 450 gm

For key to symbols — see page 7

Varieties

Varieties	Type	Variety grown	Yield, flavour & notes for next year	Expected yield
ALL THE YEAR ROUND: A very popular medium-sized variety — pale green and slow to bolt. It can be sown in spring, summer or autumn	B			
AVONDEFIANCE: The dark green heads are mildew-resistant — a good choice for June-August sowing. Slower to bolt than most Butterheads	B			
ARCTIC KING: A good one to choose if you want a lettuce for sowing during the winter months for an early spring crop	B			
BUTTERCRUNCH: The creamy heart of this American variety is unusually hard and crisp for a Butterhead. Stands for a long time without bolting	B			
MARVEL OF FOUR SEASONS: An attractive lettuce which has solid heads of frilly leaves — green edged with red. Good flavour	B			
TOM THUMB: The favourite lettuce for small plots and window boxes, producing tennis-ball heads in summer from a spring sowing	B			
CLARION: A pale green, open-hearted variety for a summer or early winter crop. Good disease resistance	B			
VALDOR: A good winter-hardy variety — Arctic King is another. Sow outdoors in late summer for a spring crop of dark green heads	B			
WEBB'S WONDERFUL: Britain's favourite Crisphead — it's in all the catalogues. Reliable, large-hearted and frilly with tightly-folded heads	C			10-20 heads from a 10 ft row
LAKELAND: An Iceberg-type of Crisphead which has been bred to be more reliable in Britain than the original Iceberg variety	C			
SALADIN: Another Iceberg-type — the heads are large and slow to bolt. The flavour is excellent and it is highly recommended	O			
FRECKLES: More open than the usual Cos lettuce, and more decorative — red-spotted green leaves. Bolt-resistant	COS			
LITTLE GEM: Compact and regarded by many as the sweetest lettuce. Small, loose heads mature quickly. Good choice for a tiny plot	COS			
LOBJOIT'S GREEN: An old favourite with dark green, self-folding leaves. Large and crisp — the most popular tall Cos	COS			
WINTER DENSITY: The No. 1 winter-hardy Cos — sow in August or September for an April crop. Heads are crisp and sweet	COS			
SALAD BOWL: An endive-like plant with leaves which are intricately cut and curled. Pick regularly. A reddish-brown variety is available	LL			
DELICATO: The cut-and-come-again lettuce to choose if you want leaves which have an oak leaf shape and a dark red colour	LL			
LOLLO ROSSA: The most popular of the red Loose-leaf varieties. Frilly, purple-edged foliage — good resistance to bolting	LL			

B	Butterhead variety
C	Crisphead variety
COS	Cos variety
LL	Loose-leaf variety

1 in. = 2.5 cm, 1 ft = 30 cm, 1 oz = 28 gm, 1 lb = 450 gm

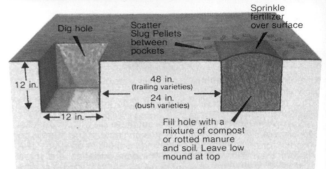

MARROW, SQUASH & PUMPKIN

All these vegetables belong to the gourd family, and only marrow is popular in Britain. In recent years courgettes (immature marrows) have become the most popular member of the group — see page 29. Marrows — large, oblong and striped, are available in both bush and trailing types. Squashes come in a variety of shapes, colours and flavours — excellent alternatives to the ordinary marrow. Summer squashes have soft skin and pale flesh — winter squashes have a hard rind and fibrous orange flesh. Pumpkins are the giants — grown for show in Britain but for other uses in the U.S.

Harvesting

Remove plants for immediate use when they are still quite small — marrows should be 8–10 in. long. They are ready when your thumbnail goes in quite easily at the stalk end of the marrow. Continual cropping is essential. For pumpkins, winter squashes and marrows for winter storage, allow the fruits to mature on the plants and remove before the frosts arrive.

See page 29 for details of seed sowing. Keep the soil moist — water copiously around the plants, not over them. Syringe lightly in dry weather. Pinch out the tips of the main shoots of trailing varieties when they reach 2 ft.

Place black polythene or a mulch around the plants before fruit formation. Once the fruits start to swell feed regularly with a liquid fertilizer. Keep marrows on a tile or sheet of glass.

Varieties

	Type	Variety grown	Yield, flavour & notes for next year	Expected yield
LONG GREEN TRAILING: Large and cylindrical with pale stripes. Grow for exhibition	M			
TIGER CROSS: Popular bush-type marrow — dark green with pale green stripes. Virus resistant. Stores well	M			
GREEN BUSH: A popular all-rounder — cut the fruits as courgettes or marrows	M			
SUNBURST: Patty pan variety — flattened yellow fruits with scalloped edges. High yields. Stores well	SS			
SCALLOPINI: Ball-shaped and scalloped-edged. Green-skinned — cook like courgettes	SS			
VEGETABLE SPAGHETTI: Flesh scrapes out in spaghetti-like strands after boiling	SS			4 marrows per plant
CROWN PRINCE: The medium-sized blue/grey fruits have orange flesh. Good nutty flavour	WS			
SWEET DUMPLING: This vigorous, trailing plant produces a plentiful supply of small creamy fruits	WS			
TURK'S TURBAN: The exotic one — acorn-shaped fruits in red, green, orange, cream etc. Yellow flesh	WS			
ATLANTIC GIANT: The one to grow for the heaviest pumpkin at the horticultural show	P			

M   Marrow variety
SS   Summer squash variety
WS   Winter squash variety
P   Pumpkin variety

Calendar

Sow outdoors in late May or early June. In the Midlands and northern areas cover the seedlings with cloches if you can for a few weeks. The first squashes will be ready in July.

For an earlier crop sow seeds under glass in late April. Plant out the seedlings in early June when the danger of frost has passed.

	JAN	FEB	MAR	APR	MAY	JUN	JUL	AUG	SEP	OCT	NOV	DEC
Recommended Sowing Time (outdoors)					■							
Actual Sowing Dates (outdoors)												
Recommended Sowing Time (under glass)				■	🌱							
Actual Sowing Dates (under glass)												
Expected Cutting Time							■	■	■	■		
Actual Cutting Dates												

1 in. = 2.5 cm, 1 ft = 30 cm, 1 oz = 28 gm, 1 lb = 450 gm

For key to symbols — see page 7

ONION & SHALLOT from sets

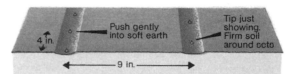

Push gently into soft earth

Tip just showing. Firm soil around sets

4 in.

9 in.

An onion set is an immature bulb which has been specially grown for planting. There are many advantages in choosing sets rather than seed. Mildew and onion fly do not attack, high soil fertility and good growing conditions are not necessary and less work is involved. An impressive list, but there are two drawbacks. Sets are a more expensive way of growing onions and there is an extra risk of running to seed (bolting). Bolting is now less of a problem than it used to be as modern varieties are more resistant than the older ones. As a further safeguard buy sets which have been heat-treated and are no larger than ¾ in. across. Shallots are milder in flavour than onions and the ones you buy are already full-sized — they quickly start to grow after planting and produce in summer a cluster of 8–12 similar-sized bulbs.

Onion sets are planted 4 in. apart — shallots require wider (6 in.) spacing. If planting has to be delayed, open the package and spread out the sets in a cool, well-lit place to prevent premature sprouting.

Protect the sets from birds if they are a nuisance in your area. Use netting rather than black thread. Keep the bed weed-free by hoeing or hand pulling. Push back any sets which have been lifted by frost or birds.

Treat as for seed-sown onions once the onion sets are established and shoots have appeared (see page 38).

Harvesting

Shallots are harvested in July when the leaves turn yellow. Lift and separate the clusters. Remove dirt and dead stems and allow the bulbs to dry. Store in nets or nylon tights in a cool dry place — the bulbs should last for about 8 months.

See page 38 for onion harvesting details.

Varieties

	Type	Variety grown	Yield, flavour & notes for next year	Expected yield
STUTTGARTER GIANT: Flat, mild-flavoured onions with good keeping qualities. An old favourite	O			
STURON: A modern variety — large, round bulbs with excellent bolt resistance	O			
AILSA CRAIG: An old favourite — round and large with white, mild-flavoured flesh	O			
NEW FEN GLOBE: A large, pale yellow and round onion. Early maturing — good keeping qualities	O			
CENTURION: An early, heavy-yielding variety. Straw colour — good for the show bench	O			7 lb from a 10 ft row
GOLDEN GOURMET: This yellow-skinned variety stores well. The shallots are large	S			
PIKANT: The skin is brown and the flavour is strong. Claimed to be bolt resistant	S			
SANTE: An exhibition and kitchen variety — bulbs are large and round	S			
HATIVE DE NIORT: The usual choice by exhibitors — perfectly shaped with deep brown skins	S			

O Onion variety
S Shallot variety

Calendar

Onion sets are planted between mid March and mid April. Shallots are planted earlier — from mid February to mid March.

	JAN	FEB	MAR	APR	MAY	JUN	JUL	AUG	SEP	OCT	NOV	DEC
Recommended Sowing Time		░	▓	░								
Actual Sowing Dates												
Expected Lifting Time							░	▓	░				
Actual Lifting Dates												

1 in. = 2.5 cm, 1 ft = 30 cm, 1 oz = 28 gm, 1 lb = 450 gm

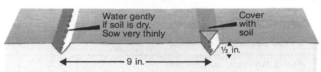

ONION from seed

Nowadays it is possible to obtain onions fresh from the garden or out of store almost all year round from a couple of carefully-timed sowings. It is not a difficult crop to care for — the secret lies in careful preparation before sowing. Choose a well-drained and sunny site — dig in autumn, incorporate compost and lime if necessary. Before sowing prepare a traditional 'onion bed'. Apply Growmore and rake over the surface when the soil is reasonably dry. Tread over the area and then rake again to produce a fine, even tilth.

Water gently if soil is dry. Sow very thinly — 9 in. — Cover with soil — ½ in.

Thin the spring-sown crop in 2 stages — first to 1–2 in. apart when the seedlings have straightened up and then to 4 in. at the small 'spring onion' stage. Lift carefully — remove thinnings which attract onion fly. Seeds of Japanese varieties should be sown 1 in. apart – thin to 4 in. spacings. Salad onion rows should be 4 in. apart.

Seedlings raised under glass should be planted 4 in. apart. Roots must fall vertically in the hole — bulb base should be ½ in. below the surface.

Hoe carefully or weed by hand. Water if the weather is dry and occasionally feed with a liquid fertilizer. Mulching cuts down the need for weeding and watering. Stop watering once the bulbs have swollen. Pull back the earth or mulch to expose the bulb surface to the sun. Break off any flower stalks which appear.

Harvesting

Pull the Salad varieties when the bulbs are ½–1 in. across — the season is between March and October. With Bulb varieties wait for about 2 weeks after the foliage has turned yellow and toppled over. Lift with a fork on a dry day. Standard Bulb onions which are not for immediate use should be dried and stored. Spread out on sacking or in trays — outdoors if it is sunny and indoors if the weather is rainy. Drying will take 7–21 days. Inspect carefully — use damaged and thick-necked ones immediately. Store sound ones in trays, net bags or nylon tights — or you can tie to a length of cord. Keep in a cool and well-lit place.

Types

STANDARD BULB varieties
&
JAPANESE BULB varieties

The Standard varieties are grown for their large bulbs which can be stored throughout the winter months. Some have a flattened shape, others are globular. Skin colours vary from almost pure white to bright red and flavours range from mild to strong. Most of them are only suitable for spring sowing but some can be sown in August for a late July crop. The Japanese varieties make late summer sowing a much more reliable routine but their midsummer crop cannot be stored.

SALAD varieties

Thinnings of the Bulb varieties can be used as salad or 'spring' onions, but there are several varieties which are grown specifically for salad use. These Salad varieties, also known as scallions or bunching onions, are white-skinned and mild-flavoured.

PICKLING varieties

Several onion varieties are grown for their small silverskin bulbs (button onions) which are lifted in July or August and pickled for use as cocktail onions. These varieties should be sown in April in sandy soil — do not feed. The seedlings should not be thinned.

Calendar

For an August or September crop sow as soon as the land is workable in the spring (late February–early April depending on the location of your garden).

Sow in mid August for an earlier crop, Japanese varieties mature in late June — Standard varieties such as Bedfordshire Champion and Ailsa Craig are less hardy, less reliable and later cropping (late July onwards), but they can be stored.

In cold areas and for exhibition bulbs sow under glass in January, harden off in March and transplant outdoors in April.

Salad onions should be sown in March-July for a June-October crop. Sow in August for onions in March-May.

	JAN	FEB	MAR	APR	MAY	JUN	JUL	AUG	SEP	OCT	NOV	DEC
Recommended Sowing Time (outdoors)		▓	▓	▓				▓				
Actual Sowing Dates (outdoors)												
Recommended Sowing Time (under glass)	🪴			🌱								
Actual Sowing Dates (under glass)												
Expected Lifting Time						▓	▓		▓	▓		
Actual Lifting Dates												

1 in. = 2.5 cm, 1 ft = 30 cm, 1 oz = 28 gm, 1 lb = 450 gm

For key to symbols — see page 7

Varieties

Varieties	Type	Shape	Variety grown	Yield, flavour & notes for next year	Expected yield
AILSA CRAIG: The one that is in all the catalogues. Very large and a show winner. Recommended for sowing under glass in January	SB				
BEDFORDSHIRE CHAMPION: Like Ailsa Craig it is large, globular and popular. It keeps much better, but it is more susceptible to mildew	SB				
RIJNSBURGER: Large and white-fleshed — the strain Balstora is a late variety with outstanding storage qualities. Onions last until May	SB				
MARCO: A globular onion with a golden brown skin. Claimed to have three advantages — high yields, early maturing and long storage life	SB				
BUFFALO: An F$_1$ hybrid which produces an early crop. Thin-necked and very hard but it is not suitable for storage	SB				
SETTON: An offspring of Sturon — see page 37. It is claimed to keep better than its parent. Golden skin — high yields	SB				
KEEPWELL: This is one to choose if you plan to sow in August. The skin is pale brown — noted for its excellent keeping quality	SB				
RED BARON: Easy to identify — the skin is dark red and inside there are white and red rings. Look for heat-treated seed	SB				
KAIZUKA EXTRA EARLY: The skin is yellow. Despite its name it is not extra early. Flattish bulbs, like most Japanese varieties	JB				
IMAI EARLY YELLOW: A straw-coloured globular or semi-globular onion which is ready for pulling in late June. Hard to find	JB				
SENSHYU: A Japanese variety which is rather similar to Imai Early Yellow, but the bulbs are flatter and it matures about 2 weeks later	JB				
WHITE LISBON: By far the most popular of the Salad varieties. Quick-growing and silvery-skinned — provides spring onions for 6 months	S				
GUARDSMAN: Stands tall and straight — hence the name. Not as popular as White Lisbon, but it has better keeping qualities	S				
WINTER WHITE BUNCHING: Sow in August or September for pulling in May. Slow to form bulbs but this variety is very hardy	S				
ISHIKURA: A distinctive type of Salad onion — the long stems do not form bulbs — pull out alternate plants and leave remainder to mature	S				
PARIS SILVERSKIN: The most popular Pickling variety. There is no need to thin — pull when the bulb is the size of a marble	P				
GIANT ZITTAU: Classed as a Pickling onion, but it will develop into a medium-sized brown bulb if you leave it in the ground to mature	P				
PURPLETTE: An early spring onion to add colour to your salads. Red-purple skin — you can leave to mature for pickling	P				

Expected yield: 8 lb from a 10 ft row

SB *Standard bulb variety*
JB *Japanese bulb variety*
S *Salad variety*
P *Pickling variety*

1 in. = 2.5 cm, 1 ft = 30 cm, 1 oz = 28 gm, 1 lb = 450 gm

Before the potato came to Britain from the New World, it was the parsnip which accompanied meat, game and fish. Nowadays it is regarded as too sweet and too strongly-flavoured to be a potato substitute, and so its popularity is low. This is a pity, as it is an easy crop to grow and there are recipes which can turn this vegetable Cinderella into a tasty dish. Any reasonable soil will do for its cultivation, but you will need deep, friable and stone-free soil if you want to grow long and tapering roots.

Harvesting

The roots are ready for cropping when the foliage starts to die in autumn. Lift as required, using a fork to loosen the soil. This lifting can continue throughout the winter, but it is a good idea to harvest and store some in November to overcome the frozen soil problem in mid winter. Lift all remaining roots in late February.

PARSNIP

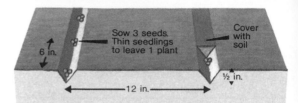

Seed is very light — sow on a still day. Germination is slow in cold weather. Parsnips seldom produce satisfactory roots after transplanting — throw thinnings away.

Hoe regularly to keep down weeds — do not touch the crowns of the plants. Very few pests attack parsnips — squash between the fingers the leaf blisters containing celery fly grubs.

Watering is required only when there is a prolonged dry spell.

Varieties

	Type	Variety grown	Yield, flavour & notes for next year	Expected yield
TENDER AND TRUE: The most popular long variety — little core plus good canker resistance	L			
HOLLOW CROWN IMPROVED: Another long one for kitchen and exhibition use. Yields are high	L			
JAVELIN: Long, slender and canker resistant. Good for the show bench	L			
COUNTESS: A smooth-skinned maincrop. Yields are good and so is the flavour. Canker resistant	L			
GLADIATOR: The first F_1 hybrid parsnip. Matures very early — good canker resistance	L			
DAGGER: Smooth skinned with good canker resistance. Noted for its tenderness	L			
WHITE GEM: Canker resistant — has taken over from the similar Offenham. Good flavour	M			
THE STUDENT: Thick and tapering — the one to choose for top flavour	M			
COBHAM IMPROVED MARROW: Tapering smooth-skinned roots. Good resistance to canker	M			
AVONRESISTER: The one for poor soils — 5 in. cones which are canker resistant	S			8 lb from a 10 ft row

L   Long variety
M   Medium-length variety
S   Short variety

Calendar

		JAN	FEB	MAR	APR	MAY	JUN	JUL	AUG	SEP	OCT	NOV	DEC
Use fresh seed every year. February is the traditional month for sowing parsnips, but it is better to wait until March. Sow short-rooted varieties in April.	**Recommended Sowing Time**												
	Actual Sowing Dates												
	Expected Lifting Time												
	Actual Lifting Dates												

1 in. = 2.5 cm, 1 ft = 30 cm, 1 oz = 28 gm, 1 lb = 450 gm

For key to symbols — see page 7

PEA

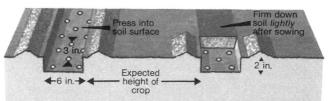

Press into soil surface

3 in.

6 in.

Expected height of crop

Firm down soil *lightly* after sowing

2 in.

If you want to taste just how good peas can be then pick the pods when the peas inside are still quite small. Within an hour boil the shelled peas for about 10 minutes in a small amount of water. Delicious, but peas are often disappointing as a garden crop. Yields can be quite small, and if the soil is poor and the weather is hot then the amount obtained may not be worth the trouble taken. The secret of obtaining a worthwhile crop is to follow the basic rules. Choose the right variety for the sowing date, make sure the soil is fertile, never sow in cold and wet soil, keep the birds away, spray when necessary, provide support as required and pick the pods at regular intervals.

Harvesting

Start harvesting when the pods are well filled but there is still a little space between each pea. Begin at the bottom of the stem and work upwards — use two hands, one to hold the stem and the other to pick off the pod. Pick regularly — pods left to mature on the plant will hasten the end of flowering and fruiting. If you harvest too many to cook immediately, place the excess in the refrigerator or deep-freeze. Pick mangetout when the pods are about 3 in. long and the peas within are just starting to develop. Asparagus peas are ready when they are 1–1½ in. long. After harvest use the stems of all pea varieties for making compost, but leave the roots in the ground.

Immediately after sowing you must protect the rows from birds. Several methods have been used over the years — black cotton stretched between short stakes, plastic netting, twiggy branches over the drills etc, but best of all are wire-mesh guards. Make sure the ends are closed.

Hoe regularly to keep weeds under control. When the seedlings are about 3 in. high insert twigs alongside the stems to provide support. You must not delay this task — leaving the stems laying on the ground will result in severe slug damage if the weather is wet. Medium- and tall-growing varieties need extra support — erect a screen of plastic netting along each row.

Water during dry spells in summer. Apply a mulch between the rows in order to conserve moisture. Pea moth is often a problem — sow a First Early variety in late March or April if it has been a problem in the past.

Types

ROUND varieties

The seeds of these varieties remain smooth and round when dried. They are all First Earlies — hardier and quicker-maturing than other types and more able to withstand poor growing conditions than the Wrinkled types. Round varieties are used for late autumn and early spring sowing.

WRINKLED varieties

The seeds of these varieties are distinctly wrinkled when dried. These 'marrowfat' peas are sweeter, larger and heavier cropping than the Round ones, and are therefore much more widely grown. They are, however, less hardy and should not be sown before March. These Wrinkled varieties are classified in two ways. Firstly by height (there are the 1½–2 ft dwarfs and the 4–5 ft tall varieties) and secondly by the time taken from sowing to first picking. First Earlies take 11–12 weeks, Second Earlies 13–14 weeks and Maincrop 15–16 weeks. In catalogues and garden centres you will find a large choice from each group.

MANGETOUT varieties

There are several types included in this group — chinese peas, snow peas, sugar snaps and eat-all. They are rather easier to grow than garden peas — pick before the seeds swell and cook the pods whole.

PETIT POIS varieties

Petit pois are not immature peas gathered from small pods of any garden pea variety — they are a small number of dwarf varieties which produce tiny (⅛–¼ in.) peas which are uniquely sweet.

ASPARAGUS PEA variety

This variety is also known as the winged pea. It is not really a pea at all — it is a vetch which produces sprawling bushy plants. It is not frost-hardy, so sowing must be delayed until May. The red flowers which appear in summer are followed by curiously shaped winged pods — these must be gathered whilst they are still small or they will be fibrous and stringy. The small pods are cooked whole like mangetout.

1 in. = 2.5 cm, 1 ft = 30 cm, 1 oz = 28 gm, 1 lb = 450 gm

PEA continued

Calendar

For a May/June Crop
Choose a sheltered site — expect some losses if the site is cold and exposed. Grow a Round variety — Feltham First is reliable for both early spring and late sowing. Meteor has an excellent reputation for hardiness. Cover seedlings and plants with cloches.

	JAN	FEB	MAR	APR	MAY	JUN	JUL	AUG	SEP	OCT	NOV	DEC
Recommended Sowing Time		▲	▲							▲	▲	
Actual Sowing Dates												
Expected Picking Time					■							
Actual Picking Dates												

For a June/July Crop
For a mid March sowing choose a Round variety or a First Early Wrinkled variety such as Kelvedon Wonder, Little Marvel or Early Onward. For late March or April sowing pick a Second Early Wrinkled type — Onward is the usual choice but Hurst Green Shaft is a good alternative.

	JAN	FEB	MAR	APR	MAY	JUN	JUL	AUG	SEP	OCT	NOV	DEC
Recommended Sowing Time			■									
Actual Sowing Dates												
Expected Picking Time						■	■					
Actual Picking Dates												

For an August Crop
Use a Maincrop Wrinkled variety — be guided by the height on the back of the packet rather than the pretty picture on the front. If space is limited choose a medium-height pea such as Senator — leave Alderman for the people who can spare 5 ft between the rows.

	JAN	FEB	MAR	APR	MAY	JUN	JUL	AUG	SEP	OCT	NOV	DEC
Recommended Sowing Time				■								
Actual Sowing Dates												
Expected Picking Time								■				
Actual Picking Dates												

For an Autumn Crop
Fresh peas are especially welcome in September and October when the main picking season is over. June-July is the sowing season and you must choose the right type — a First Early Wrinkled variety with good mildew resistance. Kelvedon Wonder will not let you down.

	JAN	FEB	MAR	APR	MAY	JUN	JUL	AUG	SEP	OCT	NOV	DEC
Recommended Sowing Time						■						
Actual Sowing Dates												
Expected Picking Time									■			
Actual Picking Dates												

Mangetout & Petit pois
Sow seeds when the soil has started to warm up in April — sowing can be delayed until May. Neither mangetout nor petit pois have become popular like the familiar garden peas — you may have to send off for seeds if your local garden shop does not carry them.

	JAN	FEB	MAR	APR	MAY	JUN	JUL	AUG	SEP	OCT	NOV	DEC
Recommended Sowing Time				■	■							
Actual Sowing Dates												
Expected Picking Time							■					
Actual Picking Dates												

Asparagus Pea
Sow seed in mid or late May so that the seedlings will appear after the last frosts have gone. Make 1 in. deep drills about 15 in. apart and sow seeds at 6 in. intervals. The harvest period usually starts at the beginning of August and continues for many weeks.

	JAN	FEB	MAR	APR	MAY	JUN	JUL	AUG	SEP	OCT	NOV	DEC
Recommended Sowing Time					■							
Actual Sowing Dates												
Expected Picking Time								■	■			
Actual Picking Dates												

1 in. = 2.5 cm, 1 ft = 30 cm, 1 oz = 28 gm, 1 lb = 450 gm

For key to symbols — see page 7

Varieties

	Type	Earliness	Variety grown	Yield, flavour & notes for next year	Expected yield
FELTHAM FIRST: 1½ ft. You will find this old favourite in all the catalogues. Needs little support — ready 11 weeks after sowing	R	1st E			
METEOR: 1 ft. The baby of the group. Very hardy — recommended for cold and exposed sites. This is the one for February sowing	R	1st E			
KELVEDON WONDER: 1½ ft. A popular variety with good mildew resistance. Suitable for both early spring and summer sowing. Pods narrow and pointed	W	1st E			
EARLY ONWARD: 2 ft. Its famous big brother (Onward) is a Second Early — this one is similar but matures about 10 days earlier	W	1st E			
LITTLE MARVEL: 1½ ft. Listed in most catalogues — a heavy cropper with blunt-ended pods borne in pairs. Useful for early sowing	W	1st E			
GRADUS: 4 ft. A tall variety amongst the First Early dwarfs. Pods are dark green, pointed and plentiful. Matures very early. Hard to find	W	1st E			
ONWARD: 2½ ft. The most popular garden pea — crops heavily and has good disease resistance. Sometimes classed as an Early Maincrop	W	2nd E			
HURST GREEN SHAFT: 2½ ft. Another popular Second Early — the pointed pods are borne at the top of the plant. Resistant to mildew	W	2nd E			
LINCOLN: 1½ ft. The pods are small but yields are abundant and the peas are very sweet. Appears in only a few catalogues	W	2nd E			
ALDERMAN: 5 ft. The giant among the Maincrops — height, yields and pod length are all large. The picking season lasts a long time	W	M			1C lb from a 10 ft row
SENATOR: 2½ ft. A Maincrop for the smaller garden. The pods are borne in pairs and the peas are noted for their abundance and sweetness. Hard to find	W	M			
OREGON SUGAR POD: 3½ ft. A popular variety listed in many catalogues. The fleshy, curved pods can reach 4-4½ in. but pick at the 3 in. stage	MT	—			
DELIKATA: 3 ft. Similar to Oregon Sugar Pod, but earlier. Mildew resistant. Pick as mangetout when pods are young. Shell peas from older pods	MT	—			
SUGAR ANN: 3 ft. This sugar snap variety is in many catalogues — it is a very early variety. Do not delay picking — older ones can be shelled for conventional peas	MT	—			
SUGAR DWARF SWEET GREEN: 3 ft. Similar to Oregon Sugar Pod — catalogues tend to list one or the other and there is little to choose between them	MT	—			
SUGAR SNAP: 5 ft. Pods are thick and fleshy. Cook as mangetout when pods are small or leave to mature and treat like french beans	MT	—			
WAVEREX: 2 ft. The most popular petit pois variety. Yield of blunt-ended pods is high — peas are tiny and very sweet	P	—			
ASPARAGUS PEA: 1 ft. A large number of small pods appear at the end of July and cropping usually continues for about 2 months	A	—			

Round variety	R	1st E	First Early garden pea
Wrinkled variety	W	2nd E	Second Early garden pea
Mangetout variety	MT	M	Maincrop garden pea
Petit pois variety	P		
Asparagus Pea variety	A		

1 in. = 2.5 cm, 1 ft = 30 cm, 1 oz = 28 gm, 1 lb = 450 gm

VEGETABLES A-Z

POTATO

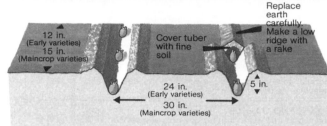

12 in. (Early varieties)
15 in. (Maincrop varieties)

Cover tuber with fine soil

Replace earth carefully. Make a low ridge with a rake

24 in. (Early varieties)
30 in. (Maincrop varieties)

5 in.

One of the advantages of growing your own potatoes is that you can choose the variety to suit you from a wide range of shapes, sizes, colours and textures. The skin may be red, yellow or white — the flesh may be white, pale cream or distinctly yellow. Texture is waxy or floury and the shape round, oval or long. This vegetable can be grown in practically any soil type — it is the best crop to grow in wasteland which is to be turned into a vegetable plot. In the established plot potatoes should not be grown on land which has been used for this vegetable within the past two seasons. Dig in autumn — liming is rarely necessary.

Seed potatoes should be the size of a small hen's egg (1-2 oz) — large seed should not be cut in half. Do not use soft or diseased ones. Set out seed potatoes in wooden trays filled with moist sand in February — eyed ends uppermost. Keep in a light frost-free place until several sturdy ¹/₂-1 in. shoots are present.

Earth-up when the stems are about 9 in. tall. Break up the soil between the rows and use a draw hoe to pile loose earth against the stems to produce a flat-topped ridge about 6 in. high. Earth-up a little at a time or do it as a one-step operation — it make no difference.

Water copiously in dry weather — this is very important once tubers have started to form.

Harvesting

Earlies are ready for harvesting when the tubers are hen's-egg size — insert a flat-tined fork into the ridge and lift roots forward. With Maincrops for storage wait until the stems have withered. Cut the stems at near ground level and remove — after 10 days lift the tubers and leave them to dry for several hours. Place in wooden boxes and keep in a dark, frost-free place.

Types

FIRST EARLY varieties
Potatoes grown for harvesting in June or July. These early-maturing varieties do not produce high yields, but they are ready when shop prices are high. They take up less space than Maincrops and are not subject to the ravages of blight. First Earlies are not generally grown for storage — lifting takes place when the tubers are quite small and they are treated as new potatoes for immediate cooking.

SECOND EARLY varieties
A small and declining group of potato varieties which bridge the gap between the First Earlies of July and the Maincrops of autumn. Sometimes called Mid-season varieties.

MAINCROP varieties
Potatoes grown for maximum yields of tubers — these potatoes are stored for winter use. Some lists separate Early Maincrops which are ready in early or mid September (Desirée, Maris Piper etc) from Late Maincrops (Golden Wonder etc) which are harvested in late September or October.

Calendar

		JAN	FEB	MAR	APR	MAY	JUN	JUL	AUG	SEP	OCT	NOV	DEC
First Early varieties: Plant seed potatoes in late March — a week or two earlier in southerly areas and a couple of weeks later in the north. Harvest in June or July. **Second Early varieties:** Plant in early–mid April and lift in July or August. **Maincrop varieties:** Plant in mid–late April. Some of the tubers can be lifted in August for immediate use but potatoes for storage should be harvested in September or early October.	Recommended Planting Time			▓	▓								
	Actual Planting Dates												
	Expected Lifting Time							▓		▓			
	Actual Lifting Dates												

Varieties

Varieties	Earliness	Shape	Variety grown	Yield, flavour & notes for next year	Expected yield
FOREMOST: White skin and white flesh. This variety has a good reputation for high yields and for staying firm when boiled	1st E				
ARRAN PILOT: White skin and white flesh. An old variety which still keeps its place in the catalogues. Tolerates dry weather better than most	1st E				
MARIS BARD: White skin and white waxy flesh. A popular First Early which is perhaps the earliest and heaviest yielder of the group	1st E				
ROCKET: White flesh. Extra early — perhaps the fastest growing potato of all. Lift when mature — do not leave it in the soil. Good for showing	1st E				
PENTLAND JAVELIN: White skin and white waxy flesh. Matures rather late but the crop is heavy and it is scab-resistant. May blacken after cooking	1st E				
HOME GUARD: White skin and white waxy flesh. An old variety dating back to World War II. Does well in heavy soils	1st E				
ESTIMA: White skin and pale yellow waxy flesh. Crops heavily and is a good chip variety. A popular choice suitable for exhibiting	2nd E				
WILJA: White skin and pale yellow waxy flesh. Another popular Dutch Second Early. Liable to blacken after cooking	2nd E				
MARIS PEER: White skin and white waxy flesh. Some resistance to scab and blight, but fails miserably in dry soil	2nd E				
CHARLOTTE: The favourite salad potato — waxy yellow flesh with a fine flavour. Golden skin — good disease resistance. Easy to grow	2nd E				
KESTRAL: White skin with purple eyes — highly recommended. Smooth-skinned — a good choice for showing. Good resistance to slugs	2nd E				
ANYA: Pink skin with waxy flesh. Bred from Pink Fir Apple — smoother skin than its parent. Salad potato with a good flavour	2nd E				
MARIS PIPER: White skin and pale creamy floury flesh. A popular successor to Majestic but scab, slug and drought resistance are low	M				Early varieties: 12 lb from a 10 ft row Maincrop varieties: 20 lb from a 10 ft row
DESIREE: Pink skin and pale creamy flesh. A good choice — heavy crops, good drought resistance and robust growth, but susceptible to scab	M				
CARA: White skin marked with pink. Renowned for its baking qualities, disease resistance and storage life. A high-yielding variety which is good for showing	M				
KING EDWARD: Red-blotched skin and creamy flesh. Good for baking. Not a heavy cropper and not immune to wart disease	M				
GOLDEN WONDER: Russet skin and yellow floury flesh. Renowned for flavour but needs good soil and good growing conditions to give a satisfactory crop	M				
PINK FIR APPLE: Pink skin and yellow flesh. The long irregular tubers have a new-potato flavour — good for potato salad. Disappointing yields	M				

1st E *First Early variety*
2nd E *Second Early variety*
M *Maincrop variety*

1 in. = 2.5 cm, 1 ft = 30 cm, 1 oz = 28 gm, 1 lb = 450 gm

RADISH

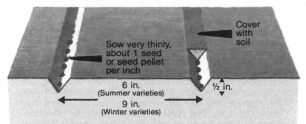

Sow very thinly, about 1 seed or seed pellet per inch

Cover with soil

6 in. (Summer varieties)

9 in. (Winter varieties)

½ in.

The popular ones are the Summer varieties which garnish the salad plate. Most (but not all) are small and the usual colour is red or a red/white mixture. There are variations — the Japanese types can grow 1 ft long and there are all-white varieties. The Winter varieties are not popular and only a few are listed in the catalogues. These have white, black or pink skins and may weigh up to several pounds. The flavour is stronger than the Summer types.

With the Summer varieties little or no thinning is required — if necessary thin to 1 in. (small radishes) or 2–4 in. (larger and Japanese radishes). Thin Winter varieties to 6 in. apart.

Protect against birds if they are a nuisance in your area. Spray with bifenthrin if flea beetles appear.

Hoe and water as necessary. Regular watering in dry weather is essential if woody and peppery roots are to be avoided.

Harvesting

Pull globular Summer varieties when they are 10p sized and medium-length ones when they are no longer than your thumb. Pull the Japanese types when they are 6 in. long. Leave Winter varieties in the ground and pull as required — cover the crowns with horticultural fleece. Alternatively lift in November and store.

Varieties

Varieties	Type	Shape & colour	Variety grown	Yield, flavour & notes for next year	Expected yield
CHERRY BELLE: Cherry-coloured on the outside — white, crisp and mild inside	S				Summer varieties: 4 lb from a 10 ft row / Winter varieties: 10 lb from a 10 ft row
SCARLET GLOBE: A quick-maturing variety — useful for early spring sowing	S				
PRINZ RUTIN: Also known as Red Prince. Remains non-woody, even when large	S				
ROUGETTE: The variety to choose for sowing under cloches in January/February	S				
SPARKLER: Bright scarlet, distinctively tipped with white. Quick growing and mild	S				
FRENCH BREAKFAST: The popular medium-length type — mild when harvested early	S				
LONG WHITE ICICLE: An excellent choice — 3 in. long radishes which are crisp and nutty-flavoured	S				
MINOWASE SUMMER: A Japanese type — can grow 12 in. long but harvest at 6 in. stage	S				
APRIL CROSS: Another Japanese or mooli type — can be sown in spring. Reaches 12 in. long	S				
CHINA ROSE: Large oval roots up to 1 lb in weight. Flesh white and crisp	W				
BLACK SPANISH ROUND: Large, black-skinned and round. Flesh is white	W				

S Summer variety
W Winter variety

Calendar

Summer varieties: Sow under cloches in January or February or outdoors in March. For a prolonged supply sow every few weeks or try 'Mixed Radish' seed which contains varieties which mature at different times. Sowing after early June often gives disappointing results.

Winter varieties: Sow in July or early August. Lift roots from late October onwards.

	JAN	FEB	MAR	APR	MAY	JUN	JUL	AUG	SEP	OCT	NOV	DEC
Recommended Sowing Time												
Actual Sowing Dates												
Expected Lifting Time												
Actual Lifting Dates												

1 in. = 2.5 cm, 1 ft = 30 cm, 1 oz = 28 gm, 1 lb = 450 gm

For key to symbols — see page 7

SPINACH

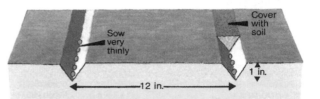

There are two types of true spinach and both are annuals. The Summer varieties have round seeds and grow quickly under good conditions to produce a tender crop throughout the summer months. The Winter varieties usually have prickly seeds and provide a useful crop of greens from October to April. The New Zealand variety is not a true spinach — it is a dwarf and rambling plant which produces mild-flavoured leaves.

New Zealand spinach needs more space than shown above. Sow 3 seeds in a group 3/4 in. deep. Leave 2 ft between the groups. Thin each group to 1 plant when the seedlings are large enough to handle.

Thin Summer and Winter varieties to 3 in. apart as soon as they are large enough to handle. Two weeks later remove alternate plants.

Hoe as necessary — water copiously in dry weather. Cover Winter varieties with cloches or straw from October onwards.

Harvesting

Start picking as soon as the leaves are a reasonable size — pick only young and tender leaves. Pick continually. With Summer varieties you can remove up to half the foliage — with Winter varieties pick much more sparingly. Remove just a few basal leaves of New Zealand spinach at each picking session.

Varieties

Variety	Type	Variety grown	Yield, flavour & notes for next year	Expected yield
KING OF DENMARK: An old favourite. Resistance to bolting is not good — choose a modern variety	S			
BLOOMSDALE: A deep green variety with reasonable resistance to bolting	S			
SIGMALEAF: Can be sown in autumn as a Winter variety. Slow to bolt	S			
BORDEAUX: The most popular variety. Dark green leaves with red stems and veins	S			
GALAXY: Leaves are dark green and shiny. Reasonably resistant to mildew	S			
PALCO: One of the modern varieties of spinach which is both mildew resistant and slow to bolt	S			
MEDANIA: A modern variety which produces an abundant supply of leaves	S			5–10 lb from a 10 ft row
SCENIC: Resistance to mildew is outstanding. Cut young upright leaves for use in salads	W			
GIANT WINTER: Noted for its hardiness and the length of its cropping season. Large, dark green leaves	W			
MONNOPA: A fine-flavoured variety which has a low oxalic acid content	W			
NEW ZEALAND SPINACH: Listed in some catalogues — flourishes in dry weather without bolting	NZ			

S Summer variety
W Winter variety
NZ New Zealand variety

Calendar

Summer varieties: Sow every few weeks from mid March to the end of May for picking between late May and the end of October.

Winter varieties: Sow in August and again in September for picking between October and April.

New Zealand variety: Sow in late May for picking between June and September.

	JAN	FEB	MAR	APR	MAY	JUN	JUL	AUG	SEP	OCT	NOV	DEC
Recommended Sowing Time												
Actual Sowing Dates												
Expected Picking Time												
Actual Picking Dates												

1 in. = 2.5 cm, 1 ft = 30 cm, 1 oz = 28 gm, 1 lb = 450 gm

For key to symbols — see page 7

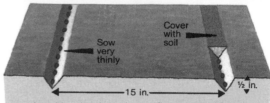

SWEDE

Swedes are closely related to turnips but the flesh is generally yellow and flavour is both milder and sweeter. In addition the plants are hardier and the yields are greater. The introduction of disease-resistant varieties has made this winter vegetable even easier to grow. All you have to do is sprinkle some seed in late spring or early summer, thin a few weeks later and then lift the large globular roots as you need them from autumn until spring.

As with other brassicas a firm, non-acid and reasonably free-draining soil is required.

Thin out as soon as the seedlings are large enough to handle. Do this in stages until the plants are 9 in. apart.

Hoe as necessary. Water copiously in dry weather – failure to do so will result in woody roots. Rain following a dry spell will cause the roots to split if the soil has not been watered.

Spray with bifenthrin at the first signs of flea beetle damage.

Harvesting

Begin lifting as soon as the roots are large enough to use. This will be from early autumn onwards — you can leave them in the soil until required. However, frozen soil in winter can be a problem so it may be more convenient to lift and store indoors in December. To store, twist off leaves and place roots between layers of moist sand in a box. Store in a cool place.

Varieties

Varieties	Variety grown	Yield, flavour & notes for next year	Expected yield
MARIAN: Purple-topped variety — the one to choose. Excellent disease resistance			
INVITATION: A breakthrough — resistant to club root as well as mildew. Purple-topped — winter hardy			
VIRTUE: A red-skinned large variety. Better flavour than the older varieties —winter hardy			
BRORA: Reputed to be the sweetest swede. Purple shiny skin. Harvest before Christmas			
BEST OF ALL: A medium-sized swede which is very hardy and stores well. Mild flavour			
ACME: A quick-growing variety — may be ready for lifting in September. The flesh is orange			30 lb from a 10 ft row
MAGRES: Round, purple-topped and mildew resistant. Fully winter hardy. The flesh is yellow			
RUBY: Listed in a number of catalogues as easy to grow. Winter hardy — mildew resistant			
MAGNIFICENT: A large-rooted variety with a good reputation for hardiness. Firm flesh			

Calendar

In order to avoid mildew it is usual to delay sowing swedes until May or early June. In dry weather water the drills before sowing.

	JAN	FEB	MAR	APR	MAY	JUN	JUL	AUG	SEP	OCT	NOV	DEC
Recommended Sowing Time					▨	▨						
Actual Sowing Dates												
Expected Lifting Time	▨	▨	▨						▨	▨	▨	▨
Actual Lifting Dates												

1 in. = 2.5 cm, 1 ft = 30 cm, 1 oz = 28 gm, 1 lb = 450 gm

For key to symbols — see page 7

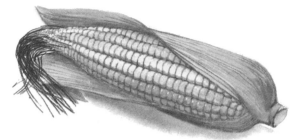

SWEET CORN

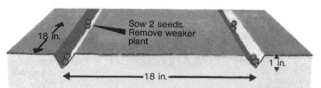

Sow 2 seeds.
Remove weaker
plant

18 in.

18 in.

1 in.

There is still a widespread view that sweet corn cannot be grown outside the southern counties, but this is no longer true. Choose one of the F₁ hybrids which have revolutionised the reliability of sweet corn in this country — the Older ('open-pollinating') varieties produce heavy crops but require a better climate than ours. Grow sweet corn in a sheltered sunny spot and the plants should not disappoint you even as far north as Lancashire or Yorkshire.

Harvesting

Test for ripeness when the silks on top of the cob have turned dark brown. Pull back part of the sheath and squeeze a couple of grains — the liquid which oozes out should be creamy but not watery. Carefully twist the ripe cob off the stem. Do this just before it is required for cooking.

Sow or plant in rectangular blocks, not in rows. This will ensure effective wind pollination of the female flowers. When raising plants under glass sow 2 seeds in 3 in. pots and take out the weaker seedling.

Remove cloches when the foliage touches the glass. Protect from birds — hoe around plants as necessary. Cover surface roots with soil — do not remove side shoots.

Water in dry weather. Stake tall plants and in summer tap the tassels at the top of each stem to aid pollination.

VEGETABLES A-Z

Varieties

Variety	Type	Variety grown	Yield, flavour & notes for next year	Expected yield
EARLY XTRA SWEET: A little later than the early ones, but very sweet	F₁			
LARK: A mid-season supersweet variety — the cobs are large and the corn is thin-skinned	F₁			
SWIFT: Another supersweet variety — the first of the thin-skinned ones. Cobs mature early	F₁			
KELVEDON SWEETHEART: Medium height — claimed to be an improvement on hard-to-find Earliking	F₁			
BUTTERSCOTCH: Noted for its tolerance of cool conditions. Mid-season variety — large cobs	F₁			
APPLAUSE: One of the modern supersweet varieties — much tastier than the older varieties	F₁			
MINIPOP: A baby corn variety. Pick as soon as the tassels are seen	F₁			
SUNDANCE: Another large-cobbed variety — a good choice in poor summers	F₁			
KELVEDON GLORY: A popular mid-season variety. Cobs are large and well-filled	F₁			
GOLDEN BANTAM: The only Older variety you are likely to find	O			1-2 cobs per plant

F₁ F₁ hybrid variety
O Older variety

Calendar

Southern counties: Sow outdoors in mid May — the cobs should be ready for picking in late August or September. For extra reliability and an earlier crop (late July onwards in mild areas) sow under glass as described below.

Other counties: Sow seeds under glass in mid April–early May and plant out in late May–early June. Alternatively sow outdoors under cloches in mid May — place cloches in position about 2 weeks before sowing.

	JAN	FEB	MAR	APR	MAY	JUN	JUL	AUG	SEP	OCT	NOV	DEC
Recommended Sowing Time (outdoors)					↓							
Actual Sowing Dates (outdoors)												
Recommended Sowing Time (under glass)				🪴	🌱							
Actual Sowing Dates (under glass)												
Expected Picking Time												
Actual Picking Dates												

1 in. = 2.5 cm, 1 ft = 30 cm, 1 oz = 28 gm, 1 lb = 450 gm

For key to symbols — see page 7

TOMATO, GREENHOUSE

Tomatoes are the main greenhouse crop in this country. It is of course extremely satisfying to pick succulent fruit from June to October, but there is a lot of work involved for the reward obtained. The plants need constant care — in summer it is necessary to water growing bags or pots at daily intervals. A wide range of pests and diseases find the tomato an ideal host and so spraying is often necessary. Still, the fascination is there and the beginner should carefully read what to do. Greenhouse varieties are cordon (single-stemmed) varieties which reach 6 ft or more if not stopped. They can be grown in border soil but it is much better to use 9 in. pots or growing bags.

Sow a couple of seeds in each 3 in. pot of compost, removing the weaker seedling after germination. Alternatively buy plants from a reputable supplier.

Plant out into growing bags, pots or border soil when the seedlings are 6–8 in. high and the flowers of the first truss are beginning to open. In border soil plant 18 in. apart.

Tie the main stem to a cane or vertical string. Cut or pinch out side shoots when they are 1 in. long. When the plants are 4 ft tall remove the leaves below the first truss. Remove yellowing leaves as the season progresses, but never overdo deleafing.

Water and feed regularly — mist plants and tap supports occasionally. Ventilate and shade in summer. When 7 trusses have set, remove tip at 2 leaves above the top truss.

Harvesting

Pick fruit when they are ripe and fully coloured. Hold the tomato in your palm and with your thumb break off the fruit at the swelling on the flower stalk. At the end of the season pick all the unripe fruit and place them as a layer in a tray. Put a couple of ripe apples next to them to generate the ripening gas ethylene. Place the tray and apples in a drawer.

Types

ORDINARY varieties
This group of red salad tomatoes contains several old favourites which are grown for reliability (Moneymaker), flavour (Ailsa Craig) or earliness (Harbinger).

F₁ HYBRID varieties
This group bears fruit which is similar in appearance to the Ordinary varieties, but these modern crosses have two important advantages — they are generally heavier yielding and also have a high degree of disease resistance.

BEEFSTEAK varieties
This group produces the large and meaty tomatoes which are so popular in the U.S. and on the Continent. They are excellent for sandwiches but only you can decide whether their flavour is superior to our familiar salad varieties. There are three types — the true 'beefsteak' hybrids such as Beefeater, the giant hybrids such as the American variety Big Boy, and the non-hybrid Marmandes (page 53), which are suitable only for outdoor growing. Stop the plants when the fourth truss has set and provide support for the fruit if necessary.

NOVELTY varieties
Catalogues sing the praises of the yellow and striped varieties but they remain distinctly unpopular. The first tomatoes sent to Europe were gold-coloured and not red, but that was a long time ago.

Calendar

In a heated greenhouse kept at a minimum night temperature of 50°–55°F, tomato seed is sown in late December and planted out in late February or early March for a May–June crop.

Most gardeners, however, grow tomatoes in an unheated ('cold') house. Sow seed in early March and plant out in late April or early May. The first fruit will be ready for picking in July.

	JAN	FEB	MAR	APR	MAY	JUN	JUL	AUG	SEP	OCT	NOV	DEC
Recommended Sowing Time (heated greenhouse)	■	⚘⚘	⚘									■
Actual Sowing Dates (heated greenhouse)												
Recommended Sowing Time (cold greenhouse)			■■		⚘⚘							
Actual Sowing Dates (cold greenhouse)												
Expected Picking Time												
Actual Picking Dates												

1 in. = 2.5 cm, 1 ft = 30 cm, 1 oz = 28 gm, 1 lb = 450 gm

For key to symbols — see page 7

Varieties

Varieties	Type	Variety grown	Yield, flavour & notes for next year	Expected yield
MONEYMAKER: Still in the catalogues, but newer varieties have taken over. Trusses are large but the flavour is bland. Fruits are medium-sized	O			
ALICANTE: Moneymaker type — heavy cropping and reliable. There are advantages — resistant to greenback and the flavour is good	O			
AILSA CRAIG: The best-flavoured variety in the Ordinary group. Fruits are medium-sized and brightly coloured. Listed in most catalogues	O			
HARBINGER: The earliest of the Ordinary varieties listed here. There are no other outstanding virtues, but flavour is good	O			
GOURMET: Another Moneymaker type of tomato, but it is more prolific and it has better disease resistance. Medium-sized fruit. Hard to find	O			
HARLEQUIN: The stems carry long trusses of plum-shaped tomatoes. No special virtues, but there is the upturned 'jester's hat' calyx on each fruit	F$_1$			
SHIRLEY: Few varieties can rival this one. Heavy yields, early crops, good disease resistance and unaffected by short cold spells	F$_1$			
HERALD: A vigorous and early-cropping variety. Tops for sweetness and flavour, according to some experts. Fruits are medium-sized	F$_1$			
NIMBUS: An early variety which can be expected to produce high yields of its medium-sized fruit. Good resistance to wilts and virus	F$_1$			
VANDOS: The yields are not particularly high and it is not disease resistant, but the thin-skinned fruits have an excellent flavour and store well	F$_1$			
SWEET MILLION: An early variety which is easy to grow. The small tomatoes are sweet and thin-skinned. The plants resist virus and fusarium wilt	F$_1$			8 lb per plant
CHERRY BELLE: A vigorous early variety which is sometimes chosen by organic gardeners because of its unusually high resistance to disease	F$_1$			
BUFFALO: Just one of a number of modern Beefsteak tomatoes. Usually bought as seedlings for potting up	B			
BRANDYWINE: This variety has been around for more than 100 years. Not the prettiest Beefsteak, but for some its flavour has not been equalled	B			
BEEFEATER: A Beefsteak variety which has several plus points. The yield is generally heavy and the picking season is prolonged. Some blight resistance	B			
FERLINE: The fruits are smaller than the ones on the other Beefsteak tomatoes, but this variety has the advantage of the best resistance to blight	B			
GOLDEN CHERRY: The cherry tomatoes on the long trusses are golden yellow and the catalogues claim that the flavour is outstanding	N			
TIGERELLA: An oddity — the fruits bear tiger stripes of red and yellow when mature. The yields are good and so is the flavour	N			

O Ordinary variety
F$_1$ F$_1$ hybrid variety
B Beefsteak variety
N Novelty variety

VEGETABLES A-Z

1 in. = 2.5 cm, 1 ft = 30 cm, 1 oz = 28 gm, 1 lb = 450 gm

TOMATO, OUTDOOR

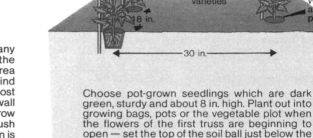

Outdoor tomatoes are not for everyone — in many areas this crop is unreliable and tomatoes need the protection of a greenhouse. But if you live in a mild area and you have a spot which is protected from the wind then you can expect a satisfactory crop in most summers. Choose a spot in front of a south-facing wall if you can. The outdoor crop is basically easier to grow than the indoor one, especially if you choose a Bush variety. Still, it is not an easy crop — regular attention is required. Remember to choose a variety recommended for growing outdoors and make sure that the soil is both free-draining and rich in humus. The tips of Cordon varieties must be removed whilst the plants are still quite small — failure to do so will prevent the tomatoes from ripening.

Choose pot-grown seedlings which are dark green, sturdy and about 8 in. high. Plant out into growing bags, pots or the vegetable plot when the flowers of the first truss are beginning to open — set the top of the soil ball just below the surface.

Loosely tie a Cordon variety to the cane. Pinch out side shoots when they are about 1 in. long. Remove yellowing leaves as the season progresses, but never overdo deleafing.

Water regularly in dry weather — if using growing bags you must water at the recommended frequency. Feed regularly. When small fruits have developed on the 4th truss remove tip at 2 leaves above this truss.

Harvesting

Follow the rules set for greenhouse tomatoes — see page 50.

Types

CORDON varieties

These varieties are grown as single stems and they have to be trimmed and supported. As described above, the stem is stopped after the 4th truss has set so as to hasten ripening before the autumn frosts. There are many red varieties, varying in size from giants to bite-sized fruits, and there are also yellow and striped tomatoes.

AILSA CRAIG
ALICANTE
SHIRLEY

Some greenhouse varieties can be grown outdoors. See page 51 for details of these dual-purpose varieties

SWEET MILLION
MONEYMAKER
TIGERELLA

BUSH varieties

These varieties make outdoor tomato growing much easier. They are either bushes 1-2 ½ ft high or creeping plants less than 9 in. tall. They do not require supporting, trimming or stopping, and are excellent for cloche culture. One drawback is that the fruits tend to be hidden, which makes harvesting more difficult than with Cordon varieties. Straw or plastic sheeting must be laid around the plants as many fruits are at ground level.

Calendar

The standard time for sowing seed under glass is in late March or early April. The young plants are hardened off during May and planted out in early June, or late May if the weather is favourable and the danger of frost has passed. Plants to be grown under cloches are planted out in the middle of May.

Under average conditions the first tomatoes will be ready for picking in mid August.

	JAN	FEB	MAR	APR	MAY	JUN	JUL	AUG	SEP	OCT	NOV	DEC
Recommended Sowing & Planting Time			▪ ▪	▪	🌱 🌱							
Actual Sowing & Planting Dates												
Expected Picking Time								▪	▪			
Actual Picking Dates												

1 in. = 2.5 cm, 1 ft = 30 cm, 1 oz = 28 gm, 1 lb = 450 gm

For key to symbols — see page 7

Varieties

Varieties	Type	Variety grown	Yield, flavour & notes for next year	Expected yield
GARDENER'S DELIGHT: Bite-sized tomatoes with a superb tangy flavour. Trusses are long and heavy. This old favourite can be grown under glass	C			
BLACK RUSSIAN: Something different. This Beefsteak tomato has deep purple skin and dark red flesh. Crops well all season long. Good flavour	C			
SUMMER SWEET: Small plum variety. Starts early with a long cropping season. Yields are high. Good wilt resistance. Can be grown under glass	C			
MARMANDE: Quite different to the ones above — the fruits are large, fleshy and irregular. These are the well-known 'Continental' tomatoes	C			
SWEET OLIVE: A popular early variety — the small, plum-shaped tomatoes are borne on long trusses. Side shoot removal is not necessary	C			
OUTDOOR GIRL: An excellent choice for outdoors — very early, high yields and good flavour. Fruits are slightly ribbed. A reliable variety	C			
SUNGOLD: Orange-red Cherry tomatoes — you will find this one in many catalogues. Very sweet flavour. Can be grown under glass	C			
THE AMATEUR: The most popular but not the best of the Bush tomatoes. A heavy cropper producing medium-sized tomatoes	B			
RED ALERT: A useful variety to grow where space is limited. Very early, bearing small fruits with an excellent flavour. Compact growth habit	B			
INCAS: A plum-shaped variety which starts to crop early in the season. Highly regarded as a culinary tomato. Good wilt resistance	B			
GLACIER: An early-cropping variety. Nothing special about its fruit, disease resistance etc — its claim to fame is outstanding tolerance to cold weather	B			
TORNADO: Well worth considering. Compact, very early and remarkably long-suffering in poor weather. Foliage is sparse but crops are heavy	B			
ROMA: Try this one for something different. Fruits are long and plum-shaped. Very meaty — good for soups and bottling	B			
TINY TIM: A dwarf variety which you can plant in a windowbox. The cherry-like fruits are bright red and almost seedless	B			
TOTEM: A British-bred variety which is recommended for growing in pots or growing bags outdoors. Dwarf, compact and early ripening	B			
TUMBLER: Very compact and easy to grow. Not a true trailer, but it is grown in hanging baskets etc and the weak stems allowed to hang downwards	T			
TUMBLING TOM RED: The first true trailing tomato. The stems are left to trail in windowboxes, baskets etc. Red Cherry tomatoes all summer	T			
				4 lb per plant

C Cordon variety
B Bush variety
T Trailing variety

1 in. = 2.5 cm, 1 ft = 30 cm, 1 oz = 28 gm, 1 lb = 450 gm

VEGETABLES A-Z

Turnips are an easy-to-grow and quick-maturing crop. The Early varieties are pulled when the roots are still young and are used in salads or for cooking — they cannot be stored. Round is not the only shape for these Earlies — there are also flat ones. There is a range of colours in the globular Maincrop varieties which are sown in summer for cropping and storage in autumn. Early turnips are more demanding than Maincrop varieties for good soil and good growing conditions.

Harvesting

Pull Early varieties when the roots are golf ball size for eating raw or snooker ball size for cooking. Begin lifting Maincrop turnips with a fork in October — in most areas you can leave the roots in the soil and lift as required. In cold and wet areas harvest the crop in early November, twist off the leaves and store the roots between layers of moist sand in a stout box.

TURNIP

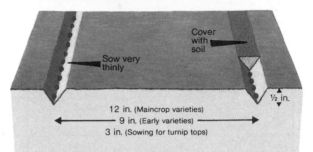

Sow very thinly

Cover with soil

½ in.

12 in. (Maincrop varieties)
9 in. (Early varieties)
3 in. (Sowing for turnip tops)

Thin out turnips when seedlings are large enough to handle. Do this in stages until plants are 9 in. (Maincrop varieties) or 5 in. (Early varieties) apart. Do not thin turnips grown for tops.

Hoe as necessary. Spray with bifenthrin at the first signs of flea beetle damage.

Water in dry weather — failure to do so can result in small, woody and cracked roots.

Varieties

	Type	Shape & colour	Variety grown	Yield, flavour & notes for next year	Expected yield
PURPLE-TOP MILAN: A popular Early — flat and reddish on top. Matures very quickly	E				
MILAN WHITE FORCING: Another Early — choose this one for growing under cloches or in frames	E				
SNOWBALL: The popular globular Early — quick-growing, white-fleshed and reliable	E				
TOKYO CROSS: Can be sown May-early September for turnips 6 weeks later	E				
RED GLOBE: A medium-sized Early. The flesh is white — the skin is red-topped	E				
ATLANTIC: Fast growing — useful for intercropping as a catch crop. Good flavour	E				
PRIMERA: A flat-topped, smooth-skinned variety. Harvest when golf ball size	E				Early varieties: 7 lb from a 10 ft row / Maincrop varieties: 12 lb from a 10 ft row
OASIS: Pure white — this variety is noted for its sweet melon-like taste	E				
MARKET EXPRESS: A late variety — quick growing. Harvest when golf ball size	M				
GREEN-TOP STONE: The variety recommended for use as spring greens. Roots are large	M				
GOLDEN BALL: The most popular and perhaps best of the Maincrops. Yellow-fleshed	M				

E Early variety
M Maincrop variety

Calendar

Early turnips: Sow Milan White Forcing under cloches in February and other Early varieties outdoors during March–June for a May–September crop.
Maincrop turnips: Sow Maincrop varieties in mid July–mid August for cropping and storage from mid October onwards.
Turnip tops: Sow a Maincrop variety in August or September for spring greens in March and April.

	JAN	FEB	MAR	APR	MAY	JUN	JUL	AUG	SEP	OCT	NOV	DEC
Recommended Sowing Time												
Actual Sowing Dates												
Expected Lifting Time				TOPS ONLY								
Actual Lifting Dates												

CHAPTER 3

CARE

BUYING SEED

When you buy a packet of seeds your interests are protected by law — there are standards of purity and germination capacity, but you must still choose carefully. You will find all the popular favourites in your local garden centre or shop, and most of these varieties have stood the test of time. For more unusual varieties you will have to turn to the mail order seed catalogues. Most of the varieties offered for sale are open-pollinated seed, which means that no specialist hybridisation has been carried out. F_1 hybrid seed is the product of crossing two pure-bred parents. Vigour and uniformity are generally increased, but so is the price.

Suppliers

Name	Comments
Local	
Mail Order	

INTERCROPPING

Remember the value of intercropping when drawing up your vegetable plot plan. Between adjacent rows of notorious slow developers such as brussels sprouts, leeks, parsnips etc a row of a fast-maturing crop is sown which will be harvested in summer before the prime crop needs the space. Popular intercroppers are radish, early peas, early carrots and dwarf lettuce. The intercropping vegetable must not make the space between the rows too narrow — if necessary widen the row spacing of the prime crop.

1 in. = 2.5 cm, 1 ft = 30 cm, 1 oz = 28 gm, 1 lb = 450 gm

GROWING UNDER CLOCHES

The sowing or planting of many vegetables under cloches can be carried out weeks earlier than on unprotected ground. This means that harvesting can take place much earlier and that will be when shop prices are high. Half-hardy crops such as capsicums can be grown successfully in less than favourable areas and leafy vegetables in winter are protected from the worst of the weather.

Choose your cloches wisely. Match the height to the expected size of the plants as the leaves should not touch the sides. Tent cloches are suitable for small plants, but you will need barn cloches for larger ones. Plastic has the benefits of lightness, safety and cheapness, but glass offers maximum clarity, stability and heat retention. To cover large areas cheaply use a plastic tunnel cloche made from wire hoops and polythene sheeting.

Provide ventilation by leaving gaps between the cloches, not by leaving the ends open. There is no need to remove the cloches before watering — the water will run down the sides and into the soil. Make sure the cloches are firmly anchored into the ground and wash the surface if it becomes grimy. Remember to increase ventilation for a few days to harden off the plants before removing their protection.

MANURING

This is the start of the gardening year. In autumn or early winter bulky organic matter is spread over the soil surface at the rate of 1 barrowload per 10 sq.yd. The area chosen should be for crops other than roots or brassicas — see page 2. This layer of organic matter is then dug into the soil. It is vital that this manuring routine is carried out so that part of the plot is enriched each year until the whole area has been treated.

Manure or fertilizer — the age-old argument. Actually there is nothing to argue about. The role of bulky organic matter is to make the soil structure good enough to support a vigorous and healthy crop. The role of fertilizer is to provide the plants with enough nutrients to ensure that they reach their full potential.

The basic (and best) materials to use are well-rotted animal manure or garden compost. Both contain the colloidal gums released by dead bacteria during the composting process. These gums produce soil crumbs and improve friability. The fibrous organic materials (coir, bark etc) are long lasting but are also less effective — they have a purely physical effect in opening up the soil and do not promote crumb formation.

Manuring Record

Name

CARE

THINNING

Despite the often-repeated recommendation to sow thinly you will usually find that the emerged seedlings are too close together. Thinning is necessary, and this is a job to be tackled as soon as the plants are large enough to handle — delay will result in spindly, weak plants which never fully recover. The soil should be moist — water if necessary. Hold down earth around the unwanted seedling with one hand and pull the plant up with the other. If the seedlings are too close together to allow this technique, merely nip off the top growth of the unwanted ones and leave the roots in the soil. After thinning, firm the soil around the remaining seedlings and water gently. This thinning is often done in stages before the final spacing is reached.

TRANSPLANTING

Transplanting involves moving seedlings to their permanent quarters. These transplants may have been raised in a seed bed in a garden, bought from a reliable supplier or grown under glass in pots or trays of compost. It is a temptation to lift thinnings in an overcrowded row of seedlings in the garden and plant them elsewhere, but you must remember that transplanting is not suitable for all vegetables. It is firmly recommended for most brassicas, acceptable for some popular crops such as peas and beans and definitely not recommended for many others such as lettuce and root crops. The rule is to check first. Water both the seedlings and the site where they are to be planted on the day before transplanting. Use a trowel (or a dibber for brassicas) to set the plants at the depth they were in the seed bed or pot. Firm the soil around the plants and water in to settle the roots. Transplanting is a critical time in the plant's life. Cold, wet soil can be fatal and so can late frosts for half-hardy vegetables. Water if there is a dry spell after planting and provide protection if birds are a habitual nuisance.

MULCHING

Mulching is an in-season method of manuring. A 1–2 in. layer of well-rotted compost or leaf mould is spread between the young plants once they are established in spring. Cultivate and water the surface to make sure that it is moist, weed-free and friable before application. The mulch will reduce water loss, increase nutrient content, improve soil structure and suppress weeds.

EARTHING-UP

There are several reasons for earthing-up — the drawing of soil towards and around the stems. Potatoes are earthed-up to avoid the tubers being exposed to light. When the haulm is about 9 in. high a draw hoe is used to pile loose soil against the stems to form a flat-topped ridge. The greens (broccoli, kale, brussels sprouts etc) are earthed-up for a different reason — soil is drawn up around the stems of well-developed plants to improve anchorage against high winds.

The stems of celery and leek are blanched (see page 27) by earthing-up. This begins with celery when it is about 1 ft high — with leeks this is done in stages, the height being increased a little at a time by drawing dry soil around the stems.

1 in. = 2.5 cm, 1 ft = 30 cm, 1 oz = 28 gm, 1 lb = 450 gm

FEEDING

There are a number of nutrients which are vital for vegetables — nitrogen for leaf growth, phosphates for root development and potash for strengthening resistance to disease and poor conditions. This group is required in relatively large amounts and compound fertilizers contain all three. You will find a statement of the nutrient content on the package.

One of the most important uses for compound fertilizers is to provide a **base dressing** just before sowing or planting. A granular or powder formulation is used, and Growmore is the old favourite. There are a number of brands which are based entirely on minerals and organics.

Crops which take some time to mature will need one or more **top dressings** during the growing season. These can be in powder or granular form, but you must take great care to keep such dressings off the leaves. It is better to use a soluble fertilizer. For maximum yields the top dressing should be balanced to the needs of the particular crop and its stage of growth. A nitrogen-rich one is used to promote leaf and/or stem growth. This is changed to a potash-rich one when fruit stimulation rather than leaf growth is required.

The big three (nitrogen, phosphates and potash) are not the only vital elements. Magnesium is required in moderate amounts and a number of others (manganese, iron, molybdenum, boron, etc) are needed in trace amounts. Manuring adds some to the soil — overliming and waterlogging lock them up.

Feeding Record

Date	Feed	Notes

WATERING

A prolonged dry spell can result in a small crop or even no crop at all. Heavy rain after drought causes the splitting of tomatoes and roots. Effective watering is the answer, and it is an art you must learn. Unfortunately, watering is usually dealt with very briefly in most handbooks on vegetable growing, but without adequate irrigation many crops will give disastrous results in a dry season.

The first step is to incorporate adequate organic matter into the soil — this increases the water-holding capacity. Next, the top 9 in. of soil should be thoroughly and evenly moist but not waterlogged at sowing or planting time. Finally, put down a mulch (see page 56) in late spring.

You will have done all you can to ensure a good moisture reservoir in your soil — the rest is up to the weather. If there is a prolonged dry spell then water will be necessary, especially for tomatoes, cucumbers, marrows, beans, peas, celery and onions.

The rule is to water the soil gently and thoroughly every 7 days when the weather is dry during the critical period. This is between flowering and full pod development for peas and beans, and from seedling to maturity for leaf crops. Apply 2 gallons per square yard when **overall watering**, and try to water in the morning rather than at midday or in the evening. Remember to water slowly and close to the base of the plants. A watering can is often used but you really do need a hosepipe if watering is not to be a prolonged chore. One of the most effective methods of watering is to use lay-flat perforated tubing between the rows. Simple… but expensive. Where there is a limited number of large plants to deal with, you would do better to use a technique known as **point watering**. This involves inserting an empty plant pot or creating a depression in the soil around each stem. Water is then poured into the pot or depression.

The main reason for failure or disappointment with growing bags is due to trying to follow the traditional technique used for watering the garden. Keeping the compost in a growing bag properly moist is a different technique, and you should follow the maker's instructions carefully.

Watering Record

Date	Notes

WEEDING

There is no single miracle cure for the weed problem — there are a number of tasks you will have to carry out. The first one begins before the crop is sown — at digging time remove all the roots of perennial weeds and bury small annual weeds by inverting each spadeful of soil. If the allotment or vegetable plot has been neglected and is a sea of grass and other weeds then you have a problem on your hands. The best plan Is to spray wIth glyphosate before soil preparation.

However thoroughly you remove weeds before sowing or planting, additional weeds will appear among the growing plants. Hoeing is the basic technique — it must be carried out at regular intervals in order to keep annual weeds in constant check and to starve out the underground parts of perennial ones. Keep away from the stems and do not go deeper than an inch below the surface.

Chemicals have a part to play, but must be used with care as they cannot distinguish between friend and foe. Use Weedol to burn off weed growth between plants — paint leaves of perennial weeds with glyphosate.

Weeding Record

Notes

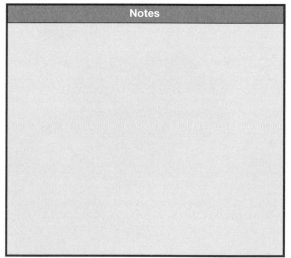

CARE

STORING

Most of the vegetables we grow are eaten shortly after picking or lifting, and that is the ideal time. Nearly all vegetables can be kept for a few days or even a week or two in the refrigerator, but if we take growing seriously then there will be times when long-term storage will be necessary. With beans there is always a sudden glut, and it is far better to pick them at the tender stage for storage rather than trying to extend the harvest period to the time when they will be tough and stringy. Maincrops of roots are generally lifted in autumn for storage indoors as layers between sand (beetroots, carrots, etc) or in sacks (potatoes) in a frost-free shed or garage. It is possible to let the vegetable plot act as the vegetable store for some roots — swedes, parsnips and turnips can be lifted as required.

Long-term storage has been completely transformed by the advent of the home freezer. This is the ideal storage method for so many vegetables, including the leafy ones which cannot be kept satisfactorily by any other method. The routine is to blanch, cool, drain and then freeze.

1 in. = 2.5 cm, 1 ft = 30 cm, 1 oz = 28 gm, 1 lb = 450 gm

PESTS & DISEASES

Leaf edges notched	Pea Bean	**PEA & BEAN WEEVIL**

End of leaves turn white	Leek	**WHITE TIP**

Leaves turn mottled, grey or brown. Fine web and minute insects on undersurface	Bean Tomato Cucumber (under glass)	**RED SPIDER MITE**

Leaves yellowish, grey or purple mould on undersurface — Cabbage family Lettuce Onion		**DOWNY MILDEW**

White blisters on leaf, containing a maggot	Celery	**LEAF MINER**

White powdery mould on leaves and stems	Pea	**PEA MILDEW**

Tiny white moth-like insects	Cabbage family Tomato	**WHITEFLY**

Small, white maggots in Peas	Pea	**PEA MOTH**

Pods distorted	Pea Bean	**THRIPS**

Small plump black insects	Bean Beet	**BLACKFLY**

Small, plump insects — green-grey, mauve or white	Cabbage family Lettuce Pea Carrot	**GREENFLY**

Holes eaten in leaves	Cabbage family	**CABBAGE CATERPILLAR**

Yellow blotches on top of leaves, purplish patches on undersurface	Tomato (under glass)	**TOMATO LEAF MOULD**

Fluffy grey or white mould on leaves and stems	General vegetable disease	**GREY MOULD**

Tubers small; plants small and weak. Poor root growth	Potato	**EELWORM**

Brown blotches on leaves	Potato Tomato	**BLIGHT**

Tubers holed	Potato	**WIREWORM MILLEPEDE**

Holes in leaves and stems	General vegetable pests	**SLUGS & SNAILS**

Soft patches on tubers. Tubers rot in store	Potato	**BLIGHT**

Stem eaten through at ground level	Cabbage family Lettuce	**CUTWORM**

Brown corky scabs on tubers	Potato	**SCAB**

Warty outgrowths on tubers	Potato	**WART DISEASE**

Underground stems and roots eaten	General vegetable pests	**WIREWORM LEATHERJACKET CHAFER GRUB MILLEPEDE SLUGS & SNAILS**

White insects on roots. Plants stop growing	Lettuce	**ROOT APHID**

Small white maggots in root	Cabbage Carrot Onion (bulb)	**CABBAGE ROOT FLY CARROT FLY ONION FLY**

Swollen root, maggots inside	Cabbage family	**CABBAGE GALL WEEVIL**

Swollen root, no maggots inside	Cabbage family	**CLUB ROOT**

1 in. = 2.5 cm, 1 ft = 30 cm, 1 oz = 28 gm, 1 lb = 450 gm

(1) TREAT PROMPTLY IF TROUBLE CAN BE CONTROLLED OR CHECKED

Pest	Control
WHITEFLY	Hang yellow Flycatcher Cards above the plants
RED SPIDER MITE	Spray with bifenthrin at first signs of attack
PEA THRIPS	Spray with insecticidal soap or pyrethrins
GREENFLY	Spray with bifenthrin or insecticidal soap
BLACKFLY	Spray with bifenthrin or insecticidal soap
SMALL CATERPILLARS	Spray with bifenthrin or thiacloprid
LEAF MINER	Pinch out and destroy affected leaflets
OTHER CATERPILLARS	Spray with bifenthrin or thiacloprid
PEA & BEAN WEEVIL	Spray with bifenthrin at first signs of attack
PEA MOTH	Sow a quick-maturing variety early in the season
CABBAGE ROOT FLY CARROT FLY, ONION FLY CUTWORM, WIREWORM MILLEPEDE LEATHERJACKET CHAFER GRUB	CABBAGE ROOT FLY: Put felt discs around stem bases ● CARROT FLY, ONION FLY: Destroy all thinnings — sow carrots thinly, use onion sets rather than seeds ● CUTWORM, WIREWORM, MILLEPEDE, LEATHERJACKET, CHAFER GRUB: Chemical treatments are no longer available. There are nematode-based insecticides for some (ask at your garden centre) but they do not work at under 50°F
ROOT APHID	Remove dead ones. Spray bifenthrin around healthy plants
SLUGS & SNAILS	Metaldehyde pellets are the traditional control measure — others such as sharp grit barriers, beer-filled saucers etc are available
CABBAGE GALL WEEVIL	No action can be recommended. Yield not seriously affected

Disease	Control
POTATO & TOMATO BLIGHT, DOWNY MILDEW	Spray with mancozeb as soon as the first symptoms are seen — repeat this treatment every fortnight as necessary
LEEK WHITE TIP	No sprays available. Do not grow leeks or onions here next year
CELERY LEAF SPOT	No sprays available. Buy 'hot water treated' seed
PEA MILDEW	Spray with sulphur at the first signs of disease
GREY MOULD	No sprays available. Always remove dead and diseased leaves
CLUB ROOT	No chemicals available. Make sure the ground is adequately limed
POTATO SCAB	Dig in compost, but do not lime before planting

CARE

(2) TAKE THE RECOMMENDED ACTION IF TROUBLE IS INCURABLE

POTATO EELWORM remains in the soil for a long time. Destroy plants and do not grow potatoes or tomatoes on the land for at least 6 years.

SOFT ROT of potatoes, turnips etc results in slimy, evil-smelling roots. Burn affected produce – in future take care not to injure roots at lifting time.

VIRUS diseases can be serious on the vegetable plot – potatoes, tomatoes and cucumbers are some of the crops at risk. There is no cure — lift and burn.

(3) CONSULT THE VEGETABLE & HERB EXPERT IF IT IS NOT LISTED

The vegetable troubles described on these two pages include most of the serious pests and diseases. There are many other problems which can occur, and some of these are nutritional or cultural disorders rather than the result of insect or fungal attack. Examples include bull-necked onions, forked carrots, bolted lettuces and blown brussels sprouts. Some of the cultural problems are shown overleaf. If your problem is not shown on page 58 or 61 consult a copy of The Vegetable & Herb Expert.

1 in. = 2.5 cm, 1 ft = 30 cm, 1 oz = 28 gm, 1 lb = 450 gm

CULTURAL CONTROL OF PESTS & DISEASES

Choose wisely. Read about the crop before you buy — don't rely solely on the seed packet. Make sure that the variety is suitable for the chosen sowing date and don't leave your purchase to the last minute — many select varieties sell out early. Sometimes you will need to buy seedlings instead of seeds for transplanting into the plot. Choose carefully — the plants should be sturdy, free from diseases and discoloration and there should be a good root system. Here you must leave it to the last minute because there should be as little delay as possible between buying and planting.

Prepare the ground properly. Good drainage is vital — a plant in waterlogged soil is likely to succumb to root-rotting organisms. Follow the rules for the correct way to manure, feed and lime the soil — remember that vegetables vary widely in their soil needs. The time for digging is autumn or early winter if you plan to sow in spring.

Get rid of weeds and rubbish. Weeds rob the plants of water, food, space and light. Rubbish, like weeds, can be a breeding ground for pests and diseases.

Rotate your crops. Soil troubles and nutrient deficiencies can build up if you grow the same crop year after year on the same site. Crop rotation is necessary for successful vegetable production — see the rules on page 2.

Avoid overcrowding. Sow seed thinly. Thin the seedlings as soon after germination as practical — overcrowding leads to crippled plants and high disease risk. Do not leave thinnings on the plot — put them on the compost heap or burn if instructed to do so.

Get rid of badly infected plants. Do not leave sources of infection in the garden. Remove and destroy untreatable plants when this book tells you to do so.

Feed and water correctly. Some plant troubles are due to incorrect feeding and soil moisture problems. Use a balanced fertilizer containing nitrogen, phosphates and potash — follow the instructions. Never let the roots get dry but daily sprinklings instead of a good soaking may do more harm than good.

CHEMICAL CONTROL OF PESTS & DISEASES

BEFORE SPRAYING: Choose the product carefully. Make sure that the problem is mentioned on the label. Insecticides should be used at the first sign of attack. A systemic insecticide enters the sap stream and so can reach insects which are hidden from the spray. Fungicides prevent rather than cure diseases, so early spraying is vital. Systemic fungicides enter the sap stream. Always read the label carefully and follow the instructions and precautions.

SPRAYING: Choose a day which is neither sunny nor windy, and choose a time in summer which is late in the day so that bees will not be harmed. Make up the spray as directed — never use equipment which has contained weedkillers. Use a fine forceful spray to cover the top and underside of the foliage — continue until the liquid starts to run off the leaves. Try to keep all sprays off the skin. If splashes occur, wash the affected area immediately.

AFTER SPRAYING: Wash out equipment thoroughly. Do this straight away — do not leave the chemical to dry inside the nozzle. Wash your hands and face if the label tells you to do so. Do not pour left-over spray into a bottle for use next time — you should make up a fresh batch of solution each time you wish to treat your plants. Store containers in a safe place away from pets and children. Never transfer chemicals into bottles — throw old containers into the dustbin after disposing of the contents safely.

Spraying Record

Date	Problem	Pesticide used	Comments

GENERAL DISORDERS

TOO LITTLE PLANT FOOD

The major plant foods are nitrogen, phosphates and potash, and a vigorous crop acts as a heavy drain on the soil's resources. Nitrogen shortage leads to stunted growth, pale leaves and occasional red discoloration. Potash shortage leads to poor disease resistance, marginal leaf scorch, and produce with poor cooking and keeping qualities. Before sowing or planting apply a complete fertilizer, such as Grow-more fertilizer, containing all the major nutrients.

One or more dressings should be applied to the growing plants. Backward vegetables are helped by using a nitrogen-rich liquid fertilizer.

WIND

Wind is often ignored as a danger, yet a cold east wind in spring can kill in the same way as frost. More frequently the effect is the browning of leaf margins. Another damaging effect is wind rock, which can lead to rotting of the roots.

FROST

A severe late frost will kill half-hardy vegetables. The shoots of asparagus and potatoes are blackened, but healthy shoots appear after the frosts have passed. The general symptoms of moderate damage are yellow patches or marginal browning of the leaves. The basic rule is to avoid sowing or planting before the recommended time unless you can provide protection. If your garden is on a sloping site, open part of the lower boundary to air movement so as to prevent the creation of a 'frost pocket'.

SHADE

In a small garden deep shade may be the major problem. Straggling soft growth is produced and the leaves tend to be small. Such plants are prone to attack by pests and diseases. Grow leaf and root types rather than fruit and pod vegetables.

TOO LITTLE WATER

The first sign is a dull leaf colour, and this is followed by wilting of the foliage. Discoloration becomes more pronounced and growth is checked. Lettuces become leathery, roots turn woody and some plants run to seed. Flowers and young fruit may drop off. If water shortage continues, leaves turn brown and fall, and the plant dies. Avoid trouble by incorporating organic matter, by watering thoroughly and by mulching.

TRACE ELEMENT SHORTAGE

Vegetables often show deficiency symptoms such as yellowing between the veins and leaf scorch. The most important trace elements are magnesium, manganese, iron, molybdenum and boron. It is not easy to tell which element or elements are lacking, and unfortunately there is no multi-element product available. Problems are most likely to occur in naturally alkaline or over-limed sandy soil, especially if the weather is dry. As a precaution make sure the soil is well supplied with compost or manure.

TOO MUCH WATER

Waterlogging affects the plant in two ways. Root development is crippled by the shortage of air in the soil. The root system becomes shallow, and also ineffective as the root hairs die. Leaves often turn pale and growth is stunted. The second serious effect is the stimulation of root-rotting diseases. Good drainage is therefore essential, and this calls for thorough autumn digging. Incorporate plenty of organic matter into heavy soil — the correct timing for humus addition depends on the crop being grown.

TOO LITTLE ORGANIC MATTER

The soil must be in good heart and this calls for liberal amounts of organic matter. Not all materials are suitable; peat may increase aeration and water retention but the need is for an active source of humus. Good garden compost and well-rotted manure are ideal. Timing is all-important — look up individual crops in this book for details.

HEAVY RAIN FOLLOWING DROUGHT

The outer skin of many vegetables hardens under drought conditions, and when heavy rain or watering takes place the sudden increase in growth stretches and then splits the skin. This results in the splitting of tomatoes, potatoes and roots. Avoid by watering before the soil dries out.

CARE

CHAPTER 4

DIARY

JANUARY

A quiet time in the vegetable garden, but you can dig if the soil is not too wet. Rhubarb can be planted now — cover established crowns with an upturned bucket to force an early crop. A few crops may be sown — leeks, onions for exhibition and tomatoes for a heated greenhouse are started this month under glass indoors — radishes can be sown outdoors under cloches.

FEBRUARY

A busier time than January, but frosty weather may make outdoor work impossible. Peas, broad beans, radishes and turnips can be sown under cloches, and greenhouse cucumbers are started indoors. Shallot planting can begin and now is the time to buy seed potatoes and set them in trays to encourage sprouting. Inspect plants for wind damage — stake if necessary.

MARCH

The vegetable year starts in earnest this month, but do not rush to sow all the early-season vegetables if the soil is still very wet and cold. March is the peak time for sowing broad beans, brussels sprouts, leeks, onions, parsnips, early peas and early turnips. It is also the month for sowing various crops under glass — capsicum, celeriac, celery, tomatoes and cucumbers.

Plant early potatoes and onion sets. Summer cabbage can be sown under cloches and so can early carrots. Top dress spring cabbage with fertilizer. Plant tomato and cucumber seedlings in pots or growing bags in a heated greenhouse.

APRIL

A peak month for sowing seed outdoors. Now is the time to put in broad beans, leaf beet, beetroot, broccoli, brussels sprouts, summer and winter cabbage, carrots, cauliflower, lettuce, peas, radishes, spinach and turnips. Finish sowing leeks, onions and parsnips.

Complete the planting of potatoes, globe artichokes and asparagus — start cutting asparagus on established beds. Sow french beans under cloches in the south, and in warmer districts plant out tomato seedlings in a cold greenhouse. A number of vegetables can be harvested this month, including late broccoli, turnip tops, spring cabbage and rhubarb. Kale and leek harvesting come to an end this month.

MAY

A busy time in the vegetable garden — sowing, planting and hoeing. Sow french beans, runner beans, beetroot, carrots, chicory, outdoor cucumber, kale, marrows, courgettes, maincrop peas, mangetout, radishes, spinach and swedes. Finish sowing broad beans, leaf beet, summer and winter cabbage, broccoli and cauliflower.

It is planting time for a number of crops — brussels sprouts, celeriac, celery, capsicum, summer cabbage and tomatoes in a cold greenhouse. Prepare the planting sites for courgettes, marrows and outdoor cucumbers — harvest early-sown lettuce and radishes.

JUNE

June is an important planting month rather than a seed-sowing one, although successional sowings of lettuces, french beans, radishes and peas continue. Finish sowing beetroot, carrots and swedes.

Vegetables for planting out include broccoli, early potatoes, brussels sprouts, sweet corn, winter cabbage, capsicum, cauliflower, celery, celeriac, leeks, courgettes, marrows and outdoor tomatoes and cucumbers — a lengthy list! Finish cutting asparagus — begin picking early-sown broad beans. Keep the plot watered if a dry spell occurs — keep watch for pest attacks. Damp down the floor and staging of the greenhouse to maintain a moist atmosphere. Apply shading to the glass.

JULY

There are numerous vegetables to harvest this month — broad beans, early-sown french beans, beetroot, greenhouse cucumbers and tomatoes, courgettes, shallots, onions, lettuce, peas, radishes, onions etc.

Sow chicory, winter radishes and maincrop turnips — continue planting lettuce and peas. Finish planting broccoli, winter cabbage, cauliflower, kale and leeks. Hoe as necessary — spray against cabbage white caterpillar and potato blight if attacks are seen. Water during a dry spell — feed with a liquid fertilizer. Pinch out side shoots on cordon tomato plants.

AUGUST

Sow winter spinach, short-rooted carrots, lettuce for an early winter crop, japanese onions, winter radishes, maincrop turnips, salad onions and spring cabbage.

There are lots of cultural jobs this month — watering, hoeing, spraying, blanching celery etc, but August is a peak month for gathering in the crops — broad beans, french beans, runner beans, leaf beet, beetroot, green broccoli, summer cabbage, capsicum, carrots, summer cauliflower, greenhouse and outdoor cucumbers and tomatoes, marrows, courgettes, onions, shallots, peas, early potatoes and globe artichokes. It is essential to harvest at the right stage — see Vegetables A-Z section.

DIARY

SEPTEMBER

Many of the vegetables which could be gathered in August can also be harvested this month, but there are additional ones — sweet corn, celery, autumn cauliflowers, brussels sprouts raised under cloches, early savoys, red cabbage and early leeks. Maincrop potatoes and carrots are lifted for storage this month. Pick tomatoes from outdoor plants and bring indoors for ripening. Plant spring cabbage.

Sow lettuce under glass for a midwinter crop or outdoors in mild districts for a spring crop. Remove shading from greenhouse glass. Cut down asparagus fern.

OCTOBER

Sow peas under cloches for a May-June crop — if you live in a mild district you can sow lettuce under cloches for spring use. Finish planting spring cabbage.

This is the great harvest month. Finish cropping french beans, runner beans, marrows, potatoes, summer cabbage, sweet corn, maincrop carrots, maincrop beetroot, greenhouse tomatoes and cucumbers, summer-sown lettuce, winter radishes and turnips. Start harvesting swedes, maincrop turnips, brussels sprouts and winter cabbage.

NOVEMBER

Cleaning up starts in earnest — begin digging. Sow broad beans in a sheltered spot and lettuce under cloches. Force chicory and cut back globe artichokes.

Harvest brussels sprouts, winter cabbage, summer-sown carrots, celeriac, celery, leeks, parsnips, swedes and turnips. November is the last month for gathering leaf beet and autumn cauliflower. Put together your seed order for next year — don't wait until the last minute.

DECEMBER

Continue digging if weather permits. Check over your tools and oil if necessary. In many gardens there is very little to gather in December apart from brussels sprouts, but in the well-stocked plot there are many vegetables to gather. These include summer-sown carrots, summer-sown lettuce under cloches, winter spinach, swedes, turnips, winter cabbage, savoys, celery, kale, chicory and leeks.